Miami Symposium on the Prediction of Behavior, 1967

Miami Symposium on the Prediction of Behavior, 1967: *Aversive Stimulation*

EDITED BY

Marshall R. Jones

UNIVERSITY OF MIAMI PRESS

Coral Gables, Florida

Contents

Preface

THE PAPERS in this volume were presented originally at a symposium held at the University of Miami in the spring of 1967. The symposium was supported in part from funds made available through a training grant from the National Institute of Mental Health to the Department of Psychology at the University of Miami.

Despite the fact that the symposium was organized around the topic of aversive stimulation, there is a wide diversity of content in the papers in this volume. Kamin reports a series of well-planned and executed experiments that sought to examine the factors which determine what elements of a compound CS are conditioned when the CS is presented in contiguity with a US, and what controls the selection of the elements which are conditioned if there are differential effects. Starting out with hypotheses concerning "attention-like" characteristics of aspects of the CS, by a series of careful, systematic steps he discovered that the relevant variables actually are somewhat related to the US. Kamin reports an impressive series of experiments, and the results are of considerable significance for theories of classical conditioning. In all probability, as Kamin himself notes, the significance of these results goes far beyond the "aversive case."

Dinsmoor reports an extensive series of experiments aimed at, among other things, the question of whether or not behavior supported by negative reinforcement can be as stable as that supported by positive reinforcement. Using a wide variety of experimental situations and several species of subjects, he presents impressive evidence that it can. He systematically explores the various advantages of the use of termination of shock for establishing conditioned responses, alternative forms of aversive stimuli that may be used, and special methods and problems encountered in studies of this type. Dinsmoor's paper is an important contribution to this widespread area of psychological research.

The paper by Bucher and Lovaas, presented at the symposium by Lovaas, reviews research using aversive stimulation such as electric shock and drug-induced nauseous reactions as a tool for behavior modification. They touch briefly on some of the ethical problems that concern this kind of treatment, and then go on to a thorough evaluation of the reported literature in this field. They note that there has been some lack of precision in this area, both in the reporting of procedures used and, especially, in the objective reporting and evaluation of the consequences of these procedures. Procedures have sometimes been applied to cases that are in continuous treatment settings, while at other times they are applied almost casually at intervals widely separated in time. Control groups are conspicuous mostly by their absence, and comparable data for alternate treatment methods are rarely reported. Bucher and Lovaas also report the results of some of their own research work, particularly with autistic children, and enliven their report with many clinical observations as well as with carefully recorded objective data. Not the least of their contribution is the brief consideration of the effect of aversive stimuli upon the person administering it. This paper should make a contribution in bringing some order into what must, at its present stage of development, be considered as a somewhat disorderly area.

On behalf of the Department of Psychology, I should like to express gratitude to the National Institute of Mental Health for the grant, to the administration of the University of Miami which encouraged this symposium in many ways, and to my colleagues in the Department for their assistance in selecting the symposium participants and making the multitudinous arrangements necessary for such a meeting.

MARSHALL R. JONES

"Attention-like" Processes in Classical Conditioning[1]

LEON J. KAMIN

McMaster University

THE EXPERIMENTS to be described have only a marginal relevance to the focus of this symposium but the studies do involve the use of aversive stimulation. The intent of the studies has been to examine the role of "attention-like" processes in conditioning. With this aim in mind, the procedure employed throughout has been the conditioned emotional response (CER), first described by Estes and Skinner (1941). Previously (Kamin, 1965), we have attempted to indicate how the CER provides an extremely sensitive and efficient procedure for the analysis of variables affecting Pavlovian conditioning in general. Thus, the results to be described, and the theoretical consequences which flow from them, are not, I am convinced, limited to the aversive case. The present results derive from rats in a CER procedure, with an electric shock unconditioned stimulus (US); but very similar results have been obtained in the McMaster laboratory by H. M. Jenkins, using pigeons in a food-reinforced operant discrimination. What appears to be involved in all of these studies is a concern with some of the phenomena, easily observable in conditioning experiments, that are usually referred to as examples of "selective attention."

The present work on "attention-like" processes arose from the use of compound CS's in a Pavlovian conditioning paradigm. The usual statement of the conditions sufficient for establishment of a Pavlovian condi-

1. This work was supported by a research grant from the Associate Committee on Experimental Psychology, National Research Council of Canada.

tioned response asserts simply that a neutral, to-be-conditioned CS must be presented in contiguity with an US. When, however, a compound CS, consisting of elements known to be independently conditionable, is presented in contiguity with a US, are all elements of the CS effectively conditioned? If not, what factors determine which elements of the CS are conditioned?

The experimental approach, in overview, was as follows. Train an animal to respond to a simple CS, consisting of Element A. Then, train the animal to respond to a compound, consisting of Element A plus a superimposed Element B. Finally, test the animal with Element B alone. Will it respond to Element B? Put very naïvely, our first notion was that, because of the prior training to Element A, this element might so "engage the animal's attention" during presentation of the compound that it would not "notice" the added Element B. The failure to notice the superimposed element might preclude any conditioning to it. To conclude that the prior training to Element A was responsible for a failure to respond to Element B we must, of course, show that animals trained to the compound without prior training to A do respond when tested with B. To control for amount of experience with the US, we ought also to show that if compound training is followed by training to A alone, the animal will respond when tested with B.

The first approach to "attention" involved this relatively simple design. The work has developed in several directions, however, and to date has utilized more than 1,000 rats as subjects, in more than 100 experimental groups. Some selected aspects of this work are summarized here.

The basic CER procedure utilized in all studies employs naïve, hooded rats as subjects, reduced to 75% of ad-lib body weight and maintained on a 24 hour feeding rhythm. The rats are first trained to press a bar for a food reward in a standard, automatically programmed, operant conditioning chamber. The daily sessions are 2 hours in length, with food pellets being delivered according to a 2.5-minute variable interval reinforcement schedule. The first five sessions (10 hours) produce stable bar-pressing rates in individual rats, and CER training is then begun. During CER training, the food reinforcement schedule remains in effect throughout the daily 2-hour sessions, but four CS-US sequences are now programmed independently of the animal's behavior. The CS, typically, has a duration of 3 minutes, and is followed immediately by a half-second US, typically a 1-milliampere shock. For each CER trial (four trials daily), a "suppression ratio" is calculated. The ratio is B/ A+B, where B represents the number of bar presses during the 3-minute CS, and A the number of bar presses during the 3-minute period immediately preceding the CS. Thus, if the CS has no effect on the animal's bar pressing, the ratio is .50; but as the CS, with repeated trials, begins to suppress bar pressing, the ratio drops toward an asymptote very close to .00. We regard the learned suppression produced by the CS as an index of an association between CS and US, much as conditioned salivation to a metronome may be regarded as such an index.

The CS, in the experiments to be described, was either a white noise (typically 80 db), the turning on of an overhead house light (7.5 w. bulb diffused through milky plastic ceiling), or a compound of noise-plus-light presented simultaneously. The normal condition of the chamber is complete darkness. The various experimental groups received reinforced CER training with various CS's in different sequences. The precise sequences of CS's are detailed in the body of this report. Typically, following the CER training, the animal was given a single test day, during which a non-reinforced CS was presented four times within the bar-pressing session. The data to be presented are suppression ratios for the first test trial. While no conclusions would be altered by including the data for all four test trials, the fact that the test CS is not reinforced means that subsequent test trials contribute relatively little to differences beween experimental groups.

The characteristic outcome of our basic training procedure is depicted in Figure 1, which presents median suppression ratios, as a function of acquisition trial, for three representative groups of subjects. The groups have been trained with either noise, light, or the compound as a CS. The major point to note at present is that after a very few trials of training all groups approach asymptotic suppression. It can also be observed that light has a slightly suppressing effect on the very first trial, so that the light group tends to acquire slightly more rapidly than the noise group. Finally, the compound group acquires significantly more rapidly than either of the others.

The first experimental approach to attention is illustrated in the design outlined below. The code letter for each experimental group is indicated at the left of the paradigm. Then, the CS employed with that group during consecutive phases of CER training is noted; "L," "N," and "LN" refer, respectively, to a light, a noise, or a compound CS. The number of reinforced trials with each type of CS is indicated in

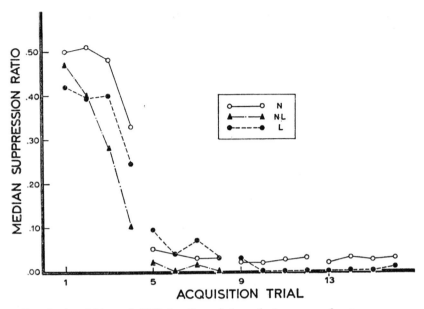

Fɪɢ. 1. Acquisition of CER by three independent groups of rats.

parentheses immediately following the CS notation; four reinforced trials are given daily. Finally, the CS employed during the test trial is indicated, together with the median suppression ratio for the group on the test trial. The number of animals per experimental group varies, in the studies to be reported, between eight and 20.

Group A:	LN (8)	N (16)	Test L	.25
Group B:	N (16)	LN (8)	Test L	.45
Group G:	....	LN (8)	Test L	.05
Group 2-B:	....	N (24)	Test L	.44

There are a number of relevant comparisons which can be made within the above set of four experimental treatments. The basic comparison is that between groups G and B. The test result for Group G indicates, as a kind of baseline, the amount of control normally acquired by the light as a result of eight reinforced, compound training trials. This is very significantly different from the result for Group B, within which the same compound training trials have been preceded by prior training to the noise element. Thus, our speculation that prior training to an element might "block" conditioning to a new, superimposed element receives support. When, however, we compare Groups A and B, we again observe a significant difference. These two groups have each received the same number of each type of CER training trial, but in a different sequence. Group B, for whom the noise training preceded compound training, is less suppressed on the test trial than is Group A, for whom the noise training followed compound training.

The fact that Group A is less suppressed than Group G is not to be interpreted as a kind of "retroactive interference" effect produced by interpolation of noise training after compound training. It must be remembered that four days elapse, for Group A, between the last compound trial and the test; appropriate control groups have established that Group A's poor performance on the test, relative to Group G's, can be attributed to the passage of time. This "recency effect," of course, works counter to the direction of the significant difference we have observed between Groups A and B. The failure of Group B to suppress to light as much as does Group A, even with a strong recency effect working to Group B's advantage, suggests a fundamental failure of conditioning to light in Group B. This is confirmed when we compare the test results of Groups B and 2-B. These groups each experience noise followed by shock 24 times, but for Group B, light is superimposed during the final eight trials. The fact that the test trial to light yields equivalent results for B and 2-B indicates that the superimpositions have produced, literally, no conditioning to the light. The test ratios for both these groups are slightly below .50, indicating again that independent of previous conditioning, an initial presentation of light has a mildly disruptive effect on ongoing, bar-pressing behavior.

While these results tended to encourage the speculation with which the experiment began, there was of course the possibility that they were specific to the particular sequence of stimuli employed. Perhaps prior training to noise blocks conditioning to light during compound training, but would prior conditioning to light block conditioning to noise? The following groups were examined in order to answer this question:

Group E:	LN (8)	L (16)	Test N	.36
Group F:	L (16)	LN (8)	Test N	.50
Group H:	. . . .	LN (8)	Test N	.25
Group 2-F:	. . . .	L (24)	Test N	.49

These four experimental paradigms are entirely analogous to those outlined previously. The sole difference is that the roles of light and noise have been interchanged, so that we are now attempting to block conditioning to noise by previous training to light. Happily, the pattern of results and significant differences in this set of four groups is identical to that observed earlier. There is, literally, no evidence for conditioning to the noise element of a compound if the animal has been previously conditioned to light alone. Thus, the blocking effect has some generality, and is not dependent on which particular stimulus is conditioned first. When we compare the present results of the noise test to those earlier reported for the light test, it is obvious that, the blocking effect aside, light tends to be the more potent member of the light-noise compound. This is consonant with our earlier observation that rats trained to suppress to light alone condition somewhat more rapidly than do rats trained to noise alone. We should stress, however, that (although we do not here present the data) we have tested many rats, after *de novo* training to the light-noise compound, to each element separately. We have never observed a rat that did not display some suppression to each element. Thus, granted the present intensity levels of light and noise, the blocking effect depends upon prior training to one of the elements; when trained from the outset to the compound, no animal "ignores" completely one of the elements.

We should also note that animals trained to noise alone after previous training to light alone acquire at the same rate as do naïve animals trained to noise alone. Prior training to noise alone also does not affect subsequent training to light alone. It seems very probable that this lack of transfer between the two stimuli, as well as some degree of equivalence between the independent efficacies of the stimuli, are necessary preconditions for the kind of symmetrical blocking effect that we have demonstrated.

The results so far presented suggest that, granted prior training to an element, no conditioning occurs to the new element that is now superimposed on the old. This might mean, as was first loosely suggested, that the animal does not "notice" the superimposed element; the kind of peripheral gating mechanism popularized by Hernandez-Peon *et al.* (1956) is an obvious candidate for theoretical service here. To speak loosely again, however, we might suppose that the animal does notice the superimposed stimulus, but does not condition to it because the stimulus is "redundant." The motivationally significant event, shock, is already perfectly predicted by the old element. The possible importance of "redundancy" and "informativeness" of stimuli in conditioning experiments has been provocatively indicated by Egger and Miller (1962). We thus decided to examine whether, in the case when the superimposed stimulus predicted something new (specifically, non-reinforcement), it could be demonstrated that the animal noticed the new stimulus. The following two groups were examined:

Group Y: N (16) LN, non-reinforced (8) N, non-reinforced (4)
Group Z: N (16)   N, non-reinforced (12)

The results for both groups during non-reinforced trials are presented in Figure 2.

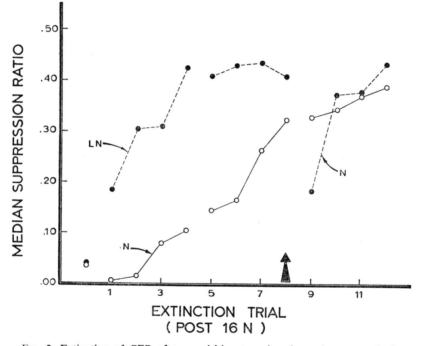

Fig. 2. Extinction of CER after acquisition to noise alone. Arrow on abscissa indicates point at which group extinguished with light-noise compound is switched to noise alone.

Through the first 16 CER training trials these groups are treated identically, and on the sixteenth trial the median ratio to noise was .02 for each group. When Group Y was presented with the compound on its next trial, its ratio increased to .18; the equivalent trial Group A, presented with the familiar noise, had a ratio of .01. The difference between groups on this trial fell short of significance but is certainly suggestive— the animals in Group Y seem to notice the superimposed light even before the compound is followed by non-reinforcement. It must be remembered that, until the moment of non-reinforcement on Trial 17, Group Y is treated identically to the "blocked" Group B in the original experiment. Thus, if this result can be replicated, we have evidence that animals do notice the superimposed element, at least on the first trial of its introduction. The evidence is in the form of an attenuation of the suppression that would have occurred had not the new element been superimposed.

To return to the comparison between Groups Y and Z, on the second non-reinforced trial Group Y's ratio was .31, Group Z's was .02. This difference was significant. Thus, a single non-reinforced presentation of the compound was sufficient for Group Y to discriminate between noise (always reinforced) and the compound (non-reinforced). The very rapid extinction in Group Y cannot be attributed to the mere failure to reinforce the noise element, as Group Z's performance makes perfectly clear. The nature of the discrimination formed by Group Y is further illustrated by comparing performance of the two groups throughout the extinction phase of the experiment. By the eighth non-reinforced trial, the ratios were .41 for Group Y and .33 for Group Z. Then, on the next trial, the stimulus for Group Y was changed to noise alone. The Group Y ratio on this trial was .17, the Group Z ratio was again .33. This was a significantly lower ratio for Group Y than had been observed on the preceding trial. Thus, to some degree, animals in Group Y had learned that it was the compound that was non-reinforced; the noise element per se had been "protected" from extinction.

We now see that, if the superimposed element provides new information, the animal not only notices the element but can utilize the information which it provides with truly impressive efficiency. Further, the attenuated suppression noted on the "transitional trial," when the new element is first superimposed on the old, suggested that, even in the earlier experiments in which the new element was redundant, the animals may have noticed it. This suggestion is confirmed by examining all of our data. We have thus far trained 153 animals with 16 trials of noise alone, followed by at least one trial of the compound. The median ratio of these animals on the sixteenth noise trial was .02; on the transitional trial (before reinforcement or non-reinforcement of the compound can exert any differential effect) the median ratio was .15. There were 106 subjects that displayed higher ratios on the transitional trial than on the sixteenth noise trial; 17 that displayed lower ratios on the transitional trial; and 30 that had equal ratios on the two trials. This is a highly significant effect.

There is thus no doubt that, at least on the first, transitional trial, an animal previously trained to a single element notices the superimposition of a new element. This observation is clearly fatal to our original theoretical notions. There remains the possibility, however, that in the case when the transitional trial proves the superimposed stimulus to be redundant, some gating mechanism comes into play at that point such that the new element is not perceived on subsequent trials. We shall return to this implausible notion a little later.

The fact that the superimposition of a new element produces an attenuation of the suppression previously learned to the old element suggests the possibility of regarding the new element as a Pavlovian external inhibitor. (When one remembers that our measure is failure to press the bar, it is obvious that the effect under discussion cannot be attributed to anything so simple as the new stimulus eliciting investigatory behavior incompatible with bar pressing.) This might encourage such questions as whether a stimulus that, at the moment of reinforcement, is acting as an inhibitor can acquire an increment in associative strength. There are, however, several considerations that seem to militate against considering the added stimulus as an inhibitor. We have examined various types of transitional trials. When an animal has first been trained to a compound, and is then presented with a single element of that compound, suppression on the transitional trial is attenuated to approximately the same degree as in the reverse case. That is, the suppression is attenuated equally whether we add an element to the old CS or subtract an element from it. The change in the old CS seems to be the controlling variable.

We now turn to an examination of some of the parameters controlling the blocking effect demonstrated in the first experiment. The fixed points from which we begin are the performances of Groups G and B. Group G, which received eight compound trials with no previous conditioning, displayed a ratio of .05 when tested to light; Group B, with 16 noise training trials preceding the eight compound trials, displayed a ratio of .45, representing a complete block of conditioning to light. What would happen if, following the 16 prior training trials to noise, a larger number of compound training trials were given? Would conditioning to the light eventually occur? This was tested in Group M, which received 24 compound training trials rather than the eight that had been given Group B. The Group M ratio, when tested to light, was .45—identical to Group B. Thus it appears that the block is not overcome by extended training to the compound. Further, during the extended block of compound training trials, the Group M animals seemed to display the asymptotic ratio characteristic of animals trained to noise alone, rather than the slightly lower asymptote characteristic of animals trained, from the outset, to the compound. Thus, the only observable effect of the light on the behavior of Group M animals was the moderate attenuation of suppression noted on the transitional trial. It is as if the animals notice the light on the transitional trial but, once the light proves to be redundant, do not notice it on subsequent trials.

What would happen if we preceded the standard eight compound trials by a smaller number of prior noise training trials than the 16 which produced a complete block in Group B? Group N received only four prior noise training trials, sufficient to produce considerable, but much less asymptotic, suppression to the noise. The ratio for Group N, tested to light following the standard compound training, was .26. This ratio is significantly higher than that for Group G, and significantly lower than that for Group B. Thus, a moderate amount of prior training to noise produces a partial block; as the number of prior training trials to noise is increased from 0 to 4 to 16, the extent of the block increases smoothly. We have since learned that eight prior training trials to noise, by which time suppression to noise is asymptotic, is sufficient to produce a complete block, and in more recent studies we have adopted eight trials of prior training as our standard procedure.

We have, as well, examined the blocking effect under a number of procedural variations that have had no effect whatever on the basic phenomenon. Thus, if the standard experiment is repeated employing a 1-minute rather than a 3-minute CS, a complete block is obtained. The same outcome is observed if the experiment is performed employing a 3-milliampere, rather than a 1-milliampere, US throughout. And again, complete blocking is obtained if the first CS, on which light onset is superimposed as a new element, is the turning off of a background 80 db noise, rather than the turning on of an 80 db noise. To put matters simply, the blocking phenomenon is robust, and easily reproducible.

When prior training to the noise element establishes the conditions necessary for demonstrating the block, can we eliminate the block by extinguishing the animal's suppression to the noise before giving it compound training? To answer this, Group O was first given four noise training trials; from Group N's performance, we know that, were we to institute compound training immediately, the final test ratio to light would be about .26. With Group O, however, the noise stimulus was at this point presented 12 times without shock, before the compound training. This was sufficient virtually to eliminate suppression to the noise before the beginning of compound training. Though suppression to the compound was learned very quickly, when tested to light alone Group O's ratio was .10—not significantly different from the baseline Group G, and significantly lower than Group N's .26. The blocking effect can thus be eliminated by teaching the animal not to respond to the previously conditioned element before inaugurating compound training. This training must take place before the compound training; Group S received four noise training trials, eight compound trials, and then 12 noise extinction trials before the test to light. The subjects showed no conditioning to the light. Thus it is not merely previous conditioning to an element that produces the block; the animal must retain its CR at the onset of compound training.

To this point in the analysis, substantial prior training to an element has given rise, invariably, to no evidence of conditioning to the superimposed element. Thus the block has appeared to be a dramatically all-or-none affair.

We now ask whether the total block that we observed in our basic Group B was in part an artifact of the relatively blunt measure of conditioning that we employed. The test trial to light, following compound training, measures transfer from the compound to the element. The savings method is known to be extremely sensitive in demonstrating transfer, much more so than is the "recall" method represented by our test. We repeated the basic experiment, but the test was no longer a single test trial to light; instead, all animals were given four reinforced training trials to light at the end of the experiment. The focus of interest is on the rate of acquisition during this training to light. The two basic groups are outlined below:

| Group 2-A: | N (16) | LN (8) | L (4) |
| Group 2-B: | . . . . | N (24) | L (4) |

While Groups 2-A and 2-B each experienced noise followed by shock 24 times before the training to light alone, the difference is, of course, that Group 2-A on the last eight trials experienced the light superimposed on the noise. Will Group 2-A therefore show any savings, relative to Group 2-B, when trained to the light alone? Or have the eight superimpositions of light literally left no effect on the animal?

There was, as our earlier results would have suggested, no significant suppression to the light by either group on the first training trial to light. However, Group 2-A displayed significantly more suppression on each of trials 2, 3, and 4 than did Group 2-B. Thus, it is clear that the eight light superimpositions did indeed leave some trace, which was manifested in a significant savings effect. However, we are reminded that our earlier data already demonstrated that, in groups trained similarly to Group 2-A, the animals did notice the superimposed light at least on the first, transitional trial. Can it be the case that the significant savings exhibited by Group 2-A is entirely attributable to the first trial on which light is superimposed? Or, do the compound trials following the first also contribute to the savings effect?

To answer this question, Group 2-N was examined. The procedure below should be compared to those diagrammed in the immediately preceding paradigm:

Group 2-N: N (16)   LN (1)   N (7)   L (4)

Group 2-N differs from Group 2-B only on the transitional trial; though the total number of reinforced experiences of noise is equated across Groups 2-A, 2-B, and 2-N, Group 2-N receives seven fewer light superimpositions than does Group 2-A. Nevertheless, the acquisition curves to light alone in the final phase of the experiment are virtually identical for Groups 2-N and 2-A; like Group 2-A, Group 2-N is significantly more suppressed than Group 2-B on each of Trials 2, 3, and 4. If we compute median suppression ratios over the four trials of light training for each group, they are .28 for each of Groups 2-A and 2-N, but .38 for Group 2-B. Thus it is clear that the savings that we have demonstrated can be entirely attributed to the first, transitional trial. We had, in any event, independent evidence that the animal noticed the light on that trial, and it is clear that the reinforcement at the termination of that trial does produce an increment in the associative connection between light and shock. There still, however, is nothing in the data that can allow us to conclude that the animal notices a redundant, superimposed element on any trial after the transitional trial; or at least we have no indication that reinforced presentations of the superimposed element after the transitional trial in any way affect either the contemporaneous or the subsequent behavior of the animal. The attention notions that prompted these studies seemed routed by the brute empirical fact of the transitional trial, but with the aid of a redundancy concept, a strategic retreat seems to have been effected, involving the surrender of only a single trial.

We turn now to a set of groups aimed at elucidating some of the temporal parameters of the blocking effect. These data, however, reflect as well on the plausibility of regarding presentation of a previously trained element as equivalent to "blotting out" or "blocking" the simultaneous presentation of an untrained element. Previous work on acquisition of the CER (Kamin, 1965) has indicated that a critically sensitive point is the moment in time when the CS and the US are literally contiguous. The introduction of a very brief gap between termination of a CS and presentation of the US adversely affects conditioning. What would be the effect of "blocking" the CS during the moment of its contiguity with the US? The paradigms aimed at this question are presented below, with a slightly modified notation to be explained in the following paragraph.

Group D:	N (16)	L (8)
Group 2-Q:	N (16)	L, + N last 5 sec. (8)
Group 2-Z:	N (16)	L, + N first 5 sec. (8)
Group 2-Y:	N (16)	L, only 175 sec. (8)
Group 3-J:	. . . . . .	L, + N last 5 sec. (8)

The first training phase outlined in the above paradigms involves no new considerations; all groups but 3-J receive the standard 16 prior training trials to noise. Group D then receives eight training trials with light. Groups 2-Q and 2-Z also receive eight training trials with light, but the noise stimulus is superimposed on the light during either the last or the first 5 seconds of the light's 180-second action. Group 2-Y, following the prior noise training, receives training trials with the light under a trace-conditioning procedure. That is, the light acts for only 175 seconds, with the shock coming, as always, 180 seconds after light-onset. Finally, Group 3-J receives the same training as Group 2-Q in the second phase, but 3-J has not had prior training to the noise. The focus of interest in this experiment is on performance during the second phase, when all groups are receiving reinforced training to the light. The light has a duration of 180 seconds for all groups but one, 2-Y, for which the light lasts 175 seconds. The acquisition data during the second phase are presented for all groups in Figure 3.

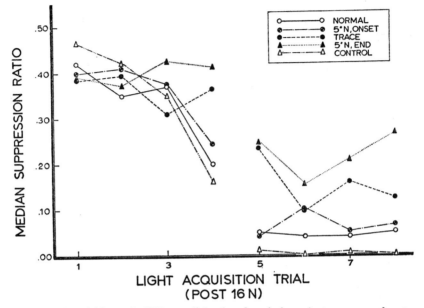

FIG. 3. Acquisition of CER to light by five independent groups of rats. Note that "control" is Group 3-J; "Normal" is Group D; "5" N, "Onset" is Group 2-Z; "5" N, "End" is Group 2-Q; and "Trace" is Group 2-Y.

The first comparison to be made is between Groups D and 2-Q. The acquisition of suppression to the light is significantly less rapid in Group 2-Q. Thus, the short burst of noise during the final 5-second action of the light does have a blocking effect. Whether a 5-second noise burst will have such a blocking effect, however, depends upon its temporal relation to the light stimulus, and to shock. Thus, Group 2-Z acquires at the same rate as Group D, significantly more rapidly than does Group 2-Q. It is only when the noise "blots out" the light at the time when light and shock are about to occur in contiguity that the blocking effect is obtained. This temporally specific blocking effect of a brief noise burst is clearly dependent on the noise's having previously been established as a CS. When, as in Group 3-J, a 5-second noise burst is superimposed over the final 5 seconds of light action from the outset of training, no blocking occurs. The rate of acquisition for 3-J is the same as that for D and 2-Z.

While Group 2-Q exhibits a temporally specific blocking effect, it must be noted that this group does acquire suppression to the light but it acquires it at a relatively slow rate. This, however, does not necessarily mean that the 5-second noise burst fails to "blot out" the light completely during the noise's action. To assess this, we require Group 2-Y. This group, following the standard initial training to noise, receives the light for only 175 seconds; the light is literally turned off during the 5 seconds preceding shock. This trace conditioning procedure produces acquisition of suppression to the light, but at a relatively slow rate; in fact, the rate is virtually identical to that observed in Group 2-Q, and is significantly slower than that in Groups, Y, 2-Z, and 3-J. Thus, exactly the same behavioral effect is produced either by turning the light off literally, or by "blotting it out" with a superimposed noise. To put it very simply, it is indeed as if the animal does not see the light when a previously trained noise-training response is acting.

The blocking effect can be shown to occur even during a training regimen that makes the superimposed stimulus logically the only correct predictor of shock. Thus, Group 3-E first received 16 training trials during which reinforced presentations of the compound were alternated with non-reinforced presentations of noise alone. This bank of 16 discrimination training trials was sufficient to produce excellent discrimination between the compound and the noise element. When Group 3-E was now tested to light alone, its ratio was .13, a very considerable suppression. The performance of Group 3-E is portrayed in Figure 4. This can be contrasted to the performance of Group 3-F, which first received 16 reinforced trials to noise alone, and then 16 discrimination training trials during which reinforced compound presentations alternated with non-reinforced presentations of the noise alone. The Group 3-F animals, as indicated in Figure 5, showed no sign whatever of discriminating between the compound and the noise element during these 16 trials. Their continued suppression during these trials is similar to what one might expect from the performance of a group that, after first being trained to noise alone on a continuous reinforcement schedule, is now shifted to a 50% partial reinforcement schedule with noise alone. Again, it is as if Group 3-F, which enters the discrimination training phase with a strongly established suppression to the noise, fails to see the light and concludes simply that the noise is now being partially reinforced. This occurs despite the fact that during discrimination training the light is the only cue that differentiates reinforced from non-

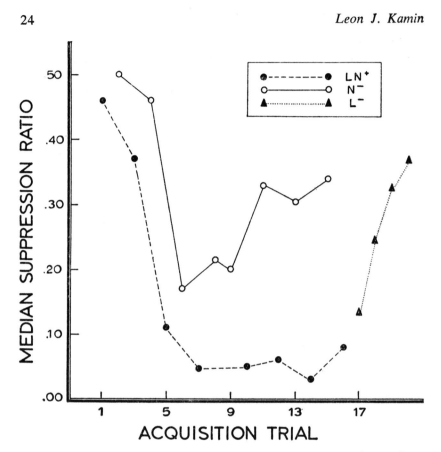

Fɪɢ. 4. Acquisition of a discriminated CER in a single group of rats. Compound trials were reinforced; noise alone trials were non-reinforced. Finally, four test trials were given to light alone.

reinforced trials. This cue was readily learned by the Group 3-E animals; however, when tested to the light alone, the Group 3-F animals showed no suppression.

To this point, our speculations about the blocking phenomenon have centered on the possibility that what is involved is, essentially, a deficit in reception of the superimposed element. The CS input is, so to speak, degraded. Perhaps, then, the block can be overcome by increasing the likelihood that the superimposed element will be attended to, e.g., by making it physically intense with respect to the prior trained element.

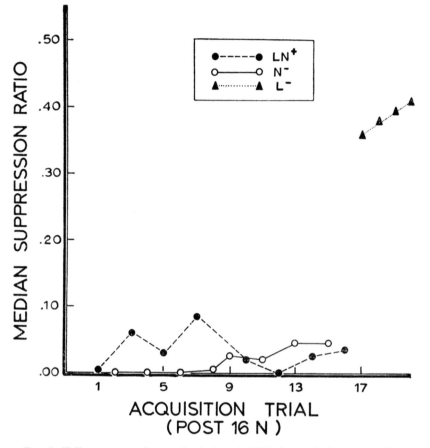

FIG. 5. Failure to acquire a discriminated CER in a single group of rats when discrimination training is given following prior acquisition to noise alone.

The next set of experiments involved first the training of different groups of animals with different noise intensities. Then each group was given compound training, with a constant light stimulus superimposed over each group's noise intensity. The question is whether the degree to which light is "blotted out" will vary with the intensity of the competing noise stimulus. The primitive notion here is that, if the block is perceptual in nature, it might be easier for a constant light stimulus to "win the animal's attention" if it is pitted against a physically weak stimulus than if it is pitted against a physically strong stimulus. The experimental paradigms are outlined below:

Group T-1:	N-50 db (16)	LN-50 db (8)	Test L	.21
Group T-2:	N-60 db (16)	LN-60 db (8)	Test L	.34
Group T-3:	N-80 db (16)	LN-80 db (8)	Test L	.42
Group T-4:	LN-50 db (8)	N-50 db (16)	Test L	.06
Group T-5:	LN-60 db (8)	N-60 db (16)	Test L	.00
Group T-6:	LN-80 db (8)	N-80 db (16)	Test L	.32

These paradigms can be viewed as a replication of the very first experiment described (demonstrating the block with Groups A and B), plus an extension of this experiment to the cases where the noise stimulus is of 50 and 60 db. The block produced in the present study by prior noise training at the 80 db level (Group T-3 vs. Group T-6) is significant, and comparable in magnitude to that demonstrated with Groups A and B. With the same type of comparison, we can demonstrate significant blocks at both the 50 and 60 db levels. But of more immediate interest, the amount of suppression during the light test is indeed a clear function of the competing noise intensity. Groups T-1, T-2, and T-3 all differ significantly from each other; the stronger the noise, the less conditioning to light occurs.

There is, however, a serious flaw in the present experiments that negates the otherwise obvious interpretation, and that at the same time suggests a fundamentally different interpretation. To begin with, the amount of suppression to noise after 16 training trials was itself a function of noise intensity. We had rather expected that Groups T-1 through T-3 would converge to a common asymptote of virtually complete suppression by the sixteenth trial of noise training, but this was not the case. The 50 db group in particular was significantly less suppressed than the others. Thus, the relatively successful conditioning to light in Group T-1 might be attributable to the relatively ineffective prior noise conditioning, rather than to the contrasting physical intensities of noises and light. We had already demonstrated that, with an 80 db noise, a partial blocking effect is produced if the prior noise training is continued for only four trials. This procedure has in common with Group T-1 the fact that, at the time when the light is first superimposed, suppression to the noise is not complete. This confounding of degree of suppression produced with physical intensity of the noise makes it foolhardy for us to view the present data as supporting a perceptual interpretation of the block.

The detailed examination of these data indicates another confounding that may be of considerable theoretical significance. We have already indicated that the level of suppression at the outset of compound training was a function of noise intensity. Further, the degree of attenuation of suppression produced by the new element on the transitional trial varied with noise intensity and, of course, with the level of suppression at the outset of compound training. Thus, the 80 db group required only one compound training trial before its suppression ratio returned to the level achieved on the last noise training trial, the 60 db group required two compound training trials, and the 50 db group seven such trials, before achieving suppression ratios as low as those obtained on the last noise training trial. These results directly parallel the amount of conditioning subsequently displayed to the light element; if suppression is minimal during the early compound trials, relatively little blocking occurs. This effect is shown quite clearly within the 50 db group, for whom a significant rank order correlation of minus .58 exists between suppression on the early compound trials and the test ratio later displayed to light. The magnitude of this correlation seems more impressive when one considers the numerous factors that might lead one to expect a positive correlation between these two measures of conditioning.

This latest observation suggests a rather different way of thinking about the blocking phenomenon. The data make it perfectly clear that, for a stimulus to be conditioned, mere temporal contiguity with the US is not sufficient. Perhaps the necessary precondition is that the stimulus be contiguous with the US during a series of trials during which the to-be-conditioned response is less than asymptotic, and thus can be conditioned. There appears to be nothing in our data that contradicts this statement. This notion implies that the degree to which the superimposed stimulus attenuates performance on the transitional trial, and on the immediately subsequent trials, is critical. The factors that determine the degree of this attenuation (external inhibition, generalization decrement, or what-have-you) may profoundly influence the degree of blocking. This line of speculation seems to be moving rather far from the naïve perceptual and "attention-like" notions with which we began. If asymptotic suppression on early compound trials is a sufficient condition for the blocking effect, there is no necessity to assume that reception of the superimposed element is in any way impeded. This in turn suggests an alternative interpretation of blocking, to which we shall return after examining a final aspect of the most recently described experiment. This final analysis involves a comparison of the original acquisition to the compound, or to the noise, of groups T-1 through T-6.

When Groups T-1 through T-3 are compared, rate of acquisition varies significantly with noise intensity; the more intense the noise CS, the more rapid is acquisition. When Groups T-4 through T-6 are compared, rate of acquisition is similarly monotonically related to the intensity of the noise element in the compound. This is not particularly surprising, but a further comparison involving the 50 db compound group is not so routine. While Group T-6 acquires significantly more rapidly than do independent groups trained to either light alone or to 80 db noise alone, and while Group T-5 acquires significantly more rapidly than do independent groups trained to either light or to 60 db noise, Group T-4 acquires at the same rate as does a group trained to light alone. Thus, although a between-group summation effect is observed by combining light with either 80 or 60 db noise in a compound, no such effect is obtained by combining light with 50 db. It is as if, even without any prior training, light completely "blots out" a weak, 50 db noise. This occurs despite the fact that 50 db is, by itself, an eminently conditionable CS. The lack of summation between 50 db and light is strikingly manifested by the behavior of Group T-4 in the second phase of the experiment. When these animals are switched from the compound to 50 db noise alone, they exhibit (unlike the 60 and 80 db groups) virtually no suppression. They must acquire to the noise element *de novo*. This result is clearly reminiscent of the "overshadowing" of a "weak" element by a "strong" element in a compound, as reported many times by Pavlov (1927, pp. 141 ff.) The question now arises whether this type of "overshadowing," which is not dependent upon prior training to one of the elements, is basically different phenomenon from the blocking effect.

There is at least one obvious way of incorporating both phenomena in the same framework. We need only assume that, during the early training trials to a compound, independent associations are being formed between each element and the US. We know, from groups trained independently with light and with 50 db noise, that the suppression to light is already asymptotic on the fifth trial, before any substantial suppression is observed in a group trained with 50 db noise. Thus, we can regard the compound group as one in which a prior training to the light element has in fact occurred before the noise element can be conditioned; the usual blocking effect then ensues. There remains, of course, the fact that all this is dependent upon the relative intensities of the noise and light elements, but the effects of various stimulus intensities may be mediated by the differential conditioning rates with which they are correlated. There thus appears to be no need to postulate different mechanisms for Pavlovian "overshadowing" and for our own blocking effect. The use of explicit prior conditioning to produce a block seems to be only another way of setting up the same chain of events that, in Pavlov's case, was set up by training from the outset to a compound consisting of "strong" and "weak" elements.

We return, in conclusion, to our most recent conception of the blocking effect, one that is no longer dependent upon the notion of a degraded CS input. To illustrate the present notion, a final experiment will be described, with the paradigms below:

Group B:	N-1 ma. (16)	LN-1 ma. (8)	Test L .45
Group 2-M:	N-1 ma. (16)	LN-4 ma. (8)	Test L .14
Group 3-U:	N-4 ma. (8)	LN-4 ma. (8)	Test L .36

The comparison between Groups B and 2-M is instructive, for here at last is a simple procedure that can eliminate the blocking effect. Within Group 2-M, shock intensity is radically increased during the compound trials. The effect of this operation is to allow the formation of a clear association between the superimposed element and the US; Group 2-M, on the test trial, is significantly more suppressed than the standard Group B. This effect is not a simple consequence of employing an intense US during the compound trials. With Group 3-U, the same intense US is employed throughout the experiment, and a clear blocking effect is manifested: the test ratio of 3-U does not differ significantly from that of B, but does from that of 2-M. Thus, it is the change of shock intensity during the compound trials from that employed during prior training that seems responsible for eliminating the block.

We can attempt to integrate the present result with our previous observation that conditioning occurred only on those compound trials when suppression was not asymptotic, in the following way. Let us suppose that, in order for an association between a CS and a US to be strengthened, it is necessary that the US "surprise" the animal. That the sudden introduction of a 4-milliampere US should be "surprising" to Group 2-M is clear enough. We can also assume, in a completely circular fashion, that whenever suppression on a compound trial is not asymptotic, the animal does not "confidently expect" the US; delivery of the US on such a trial is thus to some degree "surprising," and the result is some increment in the association between the US and whatever CS is present during the trial. That is, surprise (and thus conditioning) can occur either because the animal does not confidently expect any US at all, or because the US that in fact occurs is different in some way from that which the animal does confidently expect. This latter form of surprise is presumably operative for Group 2-M. Within the standard blocking procedure, we can assume that the attenuation of suppression observed on the transitional trial reflects the fact that superimposition of the new element has, on that trial, made the animal less than certain that the US will follow. Thus some conditioning does occur on that trial. This *post factum* reasoning seems capable of accommodating all of our previous data.

This final conception is very different from the "attention-like" notions with which we began. Perception of the CS can now be regarded as entirely intact; it is the US that is now regarded as, in a sense, "degraded." Unless the US is surprising, the "mental work" necessary for the formation of an association between the CS and the US will not be provoked. This notion that a redundant, non-informative CS will not be conditioned is clearly related to the Egger and Miller (1962) view.

The present concepts of "surprise" and "confident expectation" seem something less than fully operational, but no real difficulty seems to be involved. The fact that mere contiguity of a CS and US will not produce conditioning is overwhelmingly clear, and must be dealt with theoretically. We can regard the normal conditioning experiment as a situation in which an unpredicted US causes the animal to scan the recent stimulus input; if, and only if, this scanning occurs, an association is formed between the US and a contiguous CS. The final assumption is simply that the scanning will not occur if the US is preceded by an informative CS. Whether such a view can survive a sustained experimental attack seems highly doubtful. However, our most recent experiments involving new, independent forms of "surprise" have so far failed to dislodge it. Hopefully, with further experimentation, the concepts of surprise and informativeness can be made more operational and less circular.

REFERENCES

Egger, M. D., & Miller, N. E. Secondary reinforcement in rats as a function of information value and reliability of the stimulus. *Journal of Experimental Psychology,* 1962, **64,** 97–104.

Estes, W. K., & Skinner, B. F. Some quantitative properties of anxiety. *Journal of Experimental Psychology,* 1941, **29,** 390–400.

Hernandez-Peon, R., Scherrer, H., & Jouvet, M. Modification of electrical activity in cochlear nucleus during "attention" in unanesthetized cats. *Science,* 1956, **123,** 331–332.

Kamin, L. J. Temporal and intensity characteristics of the conditioned stimulus. In W. F. Prokasy (ed.), *Classical conditioning: a symposium.* New York: Appleton-Century-Crofts, 1965.

Pavlov, I. P. *Conditioned reflexes.* London: Oxford University Press, 1927.

Escape from Shock as a Conditioning Technique

JAMES A. DINSMOOR
Indiana University

To ILLUSTRATE the procedure used in escape conditioning, let us take a not wholly imaginary example. A rat is placed in the conditioning box, and shock is applied. When he presses the bar at one end of the box, the shock is turned off for a while. The next time the shock is presented, the rat presses more promptly than before. Because the shock must be presented before the response, in order to be turned off following the response, this form of training originally was confused with classical or respondent conditioning. But more recent analysis shows that it belongs to the operant or instrumental category. While it is the presentation of the stimulus that determines when the response will appear, it is the termination of the stimulus that determines what form it will take. With conditioned stimuli substituting for the shock, the same pattern may account for avoidance learning and for the suppression of positively reinforced behavior by punishment (Dinsmoor, 1954, 1955).

I have never conducted a formal survey to determine the relative number of studies in psychology in which positive or negative forms of reinforcement have been used, but you need only to select at random an issue of one of our research journals to find out which of these predominates. It is possible that this reflects some concensus concerning the relative importance of these two forms of control, but I prefer to think that it represents the iron grip of tradition, strengthened, perhaps, by the difficulties of this type of research, both imagined and real.

Legend has it that shock is emotionally upsetting to the subject, that it disrupts his behavior, distracts him from the problem at hand, and generally disorganizes him, thereby producing strange and puzzling results. Perhaps this impression stems partly from the early use of shock in studies of experimental neurosis, but a survey of strange behavior in animal subjects would probably reveal just as many cases when positive reinforcers were used. I, at least, find myself frequently puzzled by findings in the literature, not to mention a few in my own laboratory. It is possible that the effects produced by shock are less well understood than those produced by food, for example, but much less time and effort have thus far been expended in their analysis. Almost any type of experimentation will sometimes produce unexpected results; if this were not so, there would be little reason for conducting such investigations. But to abandon hope of bringing order out of chaos would be to abandon the scientific enterprise.

When adequate experimental control has been achieved, the patterns of behavior obtained under various schedules of reinforcement with termination of shock appear to be similar to those exhibited by animals working for more conventional reinforcers. Under a variable-interval schedule (Dinsmoor & Winograd, 1958; Dinsmoor, 1959, 1962; Dinsmoor & Bonbright, 1966), the rate is stable both locally and throughout the session except, under some circumstances, at the beginning of the session, when a positive acceleration or "warm-up" may be observed. Variable-ratio behavior (Dinsmoor & Clayton, 1963, 1966) is characteristically all-or-none, with high rates sometimes giving way to pauses, but with no intermediate values in evidence. Under fixed ratios of 5, 10, or 20, according to Winograd (1965), "performance was characterized by a brief pause before the FR was initiated, then a rapid series of responses until the shock was terminated" (p. 119). The initial pause increased with increases in the size of the ratio—i.e., the number of responses required—and decreased sharply with increases in the intensity of the stimulus. The disorderly results obtained by Weiss and Laties (1959) and by Hendry and Hendry (1963) with fixed-ratio schedules can probably be attributed to inadequate reinforcement in the first case and insufficient training in the second. Patterns of behavior appropriate to a fixed-ratio schedule were also obtained by Azrin, Holz, and Hake (1962) and Azrin, Holz, Hake, and Ayllon (1963) when monkeys were permitted to terminate a stimulus accompanied intermittently by shocks. Both fixed-ratio and fixed-interval performances have been duplicated by Morse and Kelleher (1966), using a similar arrangement, but only, it must be admitted, at the expense of using tailor-made schedules for the presentation of the shocks.

The disorganization purportedly experienced by the subject when exposed to shock has not prevented rats from forming excellent discriminations in our laboratory. In one study (Dinsmoor & Clayton, 1963), using a key-nosing response, rats were trained to respond differentially to the presence or absence of a white noise of quite moderate intensity. The shock appeared 20 seconds, on the average, before the noise, and responses occurring during this period were not effective, but the first nosing of the key in the presence of the noise terminated the shock for 60 seconds. The cumulative records presented in Figure 1 show for each

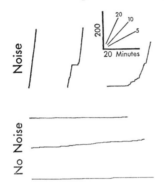

Fig. 1. Cumulative records of key nosing by each of three rats (left to right and top to bottom) in the presence and absence of white noise. Each record is composed of brief segments obtained during exposure to shock; the first nosing of the key after the onset of the noise terminated both stimuli.

of three rats the difference in performance in the presence and absence of the noise. These records were taken over a period of 5 hours of experimental time, following 110 hours of training. (Only about one-fourth of this time, however, was actually spent in the presence of shock.) The records are fairly typical of the individual performances of the three animals. Even in the poorest record, which is vitiated by a lengthy warm-up, the mean number of key nosings per minute in the presence of the noise was 34 times the rate in its absence; for the best record, the ratio was 294 to 1.

Subsequently, we trained these same rats to perform a chain of two heterogeneous responses, each on cue, to terminate the shock, as diagrammed in Figure 2. A bar was introduced at the end of the box oppo-

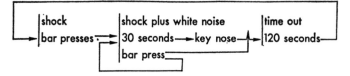

F<small>IG</small>. 2. Diagram of chaining procedure. Following onset of the shock, an average of three presses was required to turn on the noise. After 30 seconds, timed from the beginning of the noise or from the last of any bar presses occurring in its presence, nosing a key terminated both stimuli.

site to the key, and pressing was shaped by presentation of the noise; after the noise had been presented, nosing the key terminated the shock, as before. The requirements for completing the chain were then increased: a mean of three presses (VR3) was required to turn on the noise, and the shock was terminated only by the first nosing of the key after 30 seconds had elapsed since the onset of the noise (or since the last press, if the rat had pressed the bar in the presence of the noise). The rats performed the desired sequence in a highly organized manner, pressing the bar at a high rate before the noise came on during each cycle of training and nosing the key thereafter. There was very little tendency for either response to occur during the stimulus condition appropriate to the other or for either response to occur while the shock was off.

E<small>ASE</small> <small>OF</small> C<small>ONDITIONING</small>

There are even some technical advantages in using termination of shock as a reinforcer. For example, the data from several studies conducted in our laboratory indicate that most rats will readily learn to press a bar without any form of preliminary training or "shaping" of the response by successive approximation. The purpose of our first study (Dinsmoor & Hughes, 1956) was to locate appropriate parameters for rapid and reliable training.

We used two levels of shock, namely 200 and 400 microamperes (0.2 and 0.4 milliamperes), and turned off the shock for 5, 10, 20, or 40 seconds for different groups. The mean latency for the first hundred trials of the median animal in each group is presented in Figure 3. Although both the intensity and the interval criteria turned out to be statistically significant, analysis of the data from a subsequent study (Dinsmoor, Hughes, & Matsuoka, 1958) showed that most of the dif-

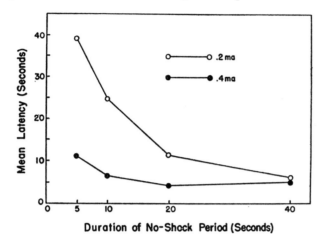

FIG. 3. Time between onset of shock and depression of bar as a function of level of current and length of time shock was interrupted following the press. Mean for first hundred trials of median rat in each group (Dinsmoor & Hughes, 1956).

ference among the groups was due to the intrusion of occasional extreme latencies rather than to a difference in the typical length of time required. That is, low intensities and short intervals produced irregularities in the animals' behavior. (See also Stavely, 1966.)

TABLE 1: Number of escape responses in initial conditioning session.

	N	range	median	pulse length (sec.)	session length (min.)
Dinsmoor & Campbell (1956a)	20	53- 80	70.0	.113	35
Dinsmoor & Campbell (1956b)	8	16-108	95.0	.113	50
Dinsmoor (1958)	20	61-128	114.5	.048	50

Data obtained from 48 rats in three subsequent experiments are presented in Table 1. In all cases, the shock was set at 200 microamperes and turned off for 20 seconds following each completed sequence of pressing and releasing the bar. Hughes (1959), also working in our laboratory, reported that 119 out of 120 rats met a criterion of 50 responses within an hour when the shock was set at 400 microamperes and termination was for 20 seconds.

The absence of any need for shaping should make the use of shock termination particularly convenient for studies in which the number of reinforcements is to be used as a parameter for the acquisition of pressing. When food or water is used as the reinforcer it is often difficult to train the animal without first reinforcing some behavior that falls short of pressing, and the effects of such reinforcements are difficult to evaluate in assessing the results. Incidentally, the ease with which we have obtained conditioning using shock cannot be ascribed to special properties of the bar or chamber that we employ, since we have experienced much greater difficulty in training rats to press the bar in the same boxes when food pellets, water, or sugar or saccharin solutions have been used as reinforcers.

TABLE 2: Median latencies in seconds on successive presentations of shock.

	1	2	3	4	5	6	7	8	9	10
Dinsmoor & Hughes (1956)	8.0	6.0	4.0	5.0	8.0	3.0	2.0	4.0	4.5	4.0
Dinsmoor & Campbell (1956a)	17.5	6.5	8.5	4.5	6.0	4.0	6.5	5.0	5.0	5.5

In two of our early studies (Dinsmoor & Hughes, 1956; Dinsmoor & Campbell, 1956a), we maintained detailed records of the time required for successive responses by each animal to the onset of the shock. Median latencies for each of the first 10 responses are presented in Table 2. They indicate that conditioning is quite rapid. The first press may take a little longer than usual, perhaps due to the slow onset of the stimulus at the beginning of the session, but the second press is already fairly typical of subsequent latencies. Some improvement may be noted later in training (Dinsmoor, Hughes, & Matsuoka, 1958; Hughes, 1959), possibly based on the learning of better preparatory behavior.

This type of conditioning can also be obtained under relatively extreme conditions. For example, Dinsmoor and Winograd (1958) were able to train rats with a shock of only 50 microamperes, later transferring them to a variable-interval, 30-second schedule and maintaining them on this routine for several hours. Dinsmoor and Clayton (1966) trained their rats from the beginning on a schedule in which a mean of three responses (ranging from one to five) was required in each instance to turn off the shock; in this study, however, a shock of 800 microamperes was employed.

One of the factors contributing to the ease with which we have been able to condition bar pressing may have been the facilitative effects of the animals' unconditioned responses to the shock. When food or water is to be used as the reinforcer, even a hungry or thirsty rat may remain

TABLE 3: Median number of presses during fifty minutes of operant level (Dinsmoor, 1958).

Deprivation Routine	Shocked	Not Shocked
Deprivation Routine	78.0	24.0
Continuous Access	57.0	15.0

relatively inactive prior to conditioning. But the initial response to shock, in our experience, includes such components as running, jumping, and rearing up against the walls of the box. In one of my experiments (Dinsmoor, 1958b), I tested the effects of both food deprivation and shock on the frequency with which the rat pressed the bar before any reinforcement was delivered. I divided the animals into four groups, two of which were placed on a cycle of 1 hour of feeding and 23 hours of fasting for ten days prior to the test session; the other two had continuous access to food. Within each pair, one group was exposed throughout the 50-minute session to a continuous shock of 400 microamperes; the other group received no shock. The results are presented in Table 3. Although the hungry animals appear to have been more active, the larger and more reliable effect was that due to the presence of the shock.

The ease of conditioning rats to press a bar, then, is not necessarily characteristic of other species or of other forms of activity which are not increased in frequency by the presentation of the shock. Hoffman and Fleshler (1959), for example, found it very difficult to shape key pecking in pigeons. "The most readily observable problem," they reported, ". . . is that the aversive stimulus elicits a variety of unlearned responses, any of which might compete with the desired behavior" (p. 214). The same kind of interpretation is supported by informal observations of the difficulty of establishing key pecking with conventional avoidance procedures.

I am reluctant, on the other hand, to agree with the second suggestion advanced by Hoffman and Fleshler that the problem arises because "the failure to terminate shock is functionally equivalent to punishment" (p. 214). The same difficulty does not seem to be encountered with other responses. Although most of our work has been based on bar pressing in rats, Marilyn Clayton succeeded in shaping several pilot and experimental rats by successive approximation to nose a pigeon key (Dinsmoor & Clayton, 1963), and James Bonbright (Dinsmoor & Bonbright, 1966) and others have trained monkeys to operate a lever. The difficulty reported by Hoffman and Fleshler may well be specific to the pigeon and the key; the same authors were able to condition head-raising by using a succession of small steps to approach the final result.

Ease of conditioning is not the only advantage to be gained by using termination of shock as a reinforcer. No deprivation of food or water seems to be required, for example, to maintain adequate levels of performance. If higher rates are desired, it is a simple matter to in-

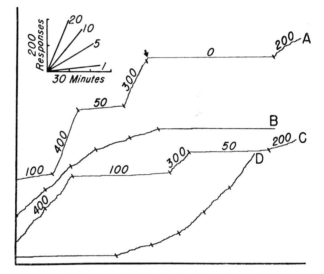

FIG. 4. Four cumulative records illustrating immediacy of changes in rate of pressing following shifts in level of shock. Numbers indicate current in microamperes. Record B represents an ascending sequence, D a descending sequence (Dinsmoor & Winograd, 1958).

crease the intensity of the shock. The cumulative records presented in Figure 4 were produced during 6-hour sessions in which the shock could be terminated for 120 seconds on a variable-interval schedule (Dinsmoor & Winograd, 1958). For record B we used a descending sequence of shock intensities for 1 hour each of experimental time, for record D an ascending sequence, and for records A and C irregular sequences designed to bring out the immediacy of the change in performance. The numbers next to each segment indicate the level of current in microamperes.

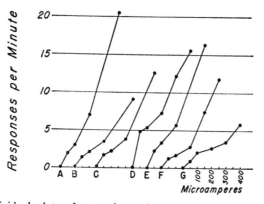

Fig. 5. Individual plots of rate of pressing as a function of level of shock. The first point in each plot represents the animal's performance at zero current, and each grid mark represents an increment of 50 microamperes (Dinsmoor & Winograd, 1958).

The functional relationship between level of shock and rate of responding is plotted for several different animals in Figure 5, taken from the same study. Each unit along the baseline represents an increment of 50 microamperes from the point at which the individual plot begins.

When shock is used to maintain the desired level of activity, the animals can be given free access both to food and to water. For short-term studies, this enables the experimenter to dispense with the usual practice of placing his animals on a feeding rhythm for several days prior to the experiment proper. For longer-term studies, elimination of the feeding schedule frees the experimenter from a form of enslavement that, in time, can become quite onerous, despite its ostensibly voluntary nature. Although some difference may occasionally be detected in the animal's behavior following the omission of a daily session, it is easy to re-establish a baseline performance or to eliminate this factor from the data to be compared. For tests of retention, special precautions are no longer required to prevent time from being confounded with level of deprivation.

A related advantage in using termination of shock as the reinforcer is that the animal never satiates. While we have found it advisable, in some instances, to use relatively long shock-free periods, of the order of 1 to 4 minutes, there is no apparent limit on the number of rein- forcements that may be delivered in a single, continuous session. Some of our experimental sessions have lasted as long as 10 hours. This in- creases the flexibility with which laboratory personnel may arrange their daily schedules and reduces the time spent inserting and removing the animals.

HOLDING

The most striking peculiarity that we noted when we began our work on escape training (Dinsmoor & Hughes, 1956) was that our rats con- tinued to hold the bar down for longer and longer periods as their training progressed, even though the initial depression was sufficient to terminate the shock. Often this meant that they were still holding the bar when the shock returned on its next presentation. Eventually they came to spend more of their time on the bar during the period between the shocks than off it.

The same type of behavior had been noted in a study by Keller (1941) in which light was used as the stimulus. In attempting to ac- count for this behavior, Keller suggested (p. 246) that the reason the same phenomenon had not been observed in other studies was that when the food was used as the reinforcer, pressing was not the final member of the chain. The animal had to release the bar in order to approach the food tray and seize the pellet. Presumably this require- ment maintained a greater tendency to release the bar once it had been pressed.

Keller's analysis indicated that it should be possible to eliminate hold- ing behavior in escape training by adding a similar requirement, i.e., by withholding the reinforcement until the animal had released the bar. Accordingly, in our second study (Dinsmoor, Hughes, & Matsuoka, 1958), we included a direct test of this measure. The rats in two of our groups were required only to press the bar in order to terminate the shock, but the rats in two comparable groups were required first to press the bar and then to release it. As may be seen in Figure 6, the added requirement did reduce the length of the initial hold following each presentation of the shock. The figure presents pooled cumulative frequency distributions for the members of each of the four groups during the last 10 trials of training. The numbers next to each distribu-

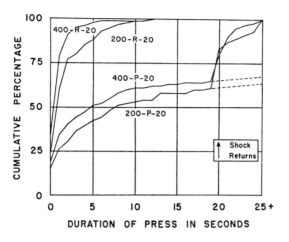

FIG. 6. Cumulative frequency distributions for duration of initial depression of bar following onset of shock. Animals in groups 400-P-20 and 200-P-20 were required only to press the bar to terminate the shock, but animals in groups 400-R-20 and 200-R-20 were required also to release it.

tion represent the level of shock in microamperes and the length of the interval in seconds between shocks. It will be noted that the rats in the press groups, 400-P-20 and 200-P-20, held more than a third of their initial presses until the return of the shock, 20 seconds later; but the rats in the release groups, 400-R-20 and 200-R-20, held the bar for a median duration of less than 1 second.

This, however, did not eliminate the problem of holding. Other data showed that the animals frequently returned to the bar after they had released it. As may be seen in Figure 7, the frequency with which the rats were found to be holding the bar at the end of the 20-second interval increased during training, even though this was accompanied by the return of the shock. All in all, the members of the press groups spent means of 65.1% and 53.4%, respectively, of their time on the bar during the interval between the shocks; the members of the release groups spent 35.4% and 29.7% of their time on the bar.

Although these data did indicate that holding was reduced by using the release procedure, this finding was not confirmed in a subsequent study in our laboratory. Using the same apparatus, Campbell (1962) found that by the end of a somewhat longer period of training his release animals were on the bar 88.1% of the time when the shock returned, while his press animals were on the bar only 75.9% of the

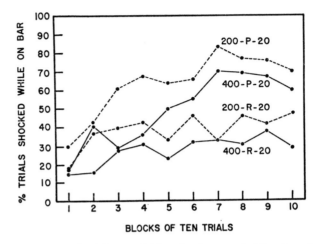

Fig. 7. Percentage of trials on which animals were holding bar down when shock returned.

time. These data indicated that the action that was followed by termination of the shock did not govern the position the animal would take in the period between the shocks. Some other factor must be involved.

Fortunately, Campbell's work also provided a new lead concerning another possible source of this type of behavior. Analyzing the sequence of events on successive trials for each animal, he found that under both procedures his rats pressed the bar sooner following the onset of shock, and hence terminated the shock more quickly, when they had been holding than when they had been off the bar. This indicated that taking a position on the bar served as a preparatory response that enabled more rapid termination of the shock. Presumably this preparatory response was maintained either because it led more quickly to the reinforcing state of affairs or because it reduced the duration, and hence the punishing effect, of the ensuing shock.

At this point, however, the evidence supporting the analysis of holding as a preparatory response was relatively weak since it was based on a correlation between two dependent variables. In order to subject this analysis to experimental test, Dinsmoor, Matsuoka, and Winograd (1958) employed two procedures designed to change the relationship between holding and the subsequent termination of the shock. The two experiments will be treated separately. In the first experiment, the manipulation was indirect: we changed the requirements for termination of the shock in such a way as to increase the magnitude of the advantage to be gained by holding. The requirements imposed in this and earlier experiments can be seen by comparing the hypothetical records presented in Figure 8. Time flows from left to right. For each pro-

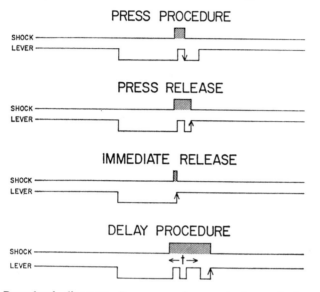

Fig. 8. Procedural diagrams. Press procedure: animal required to release bar if holding when shock begins, then press. Press release: release required following press. Immediate release: initial release effective. Delay procedure: response ineffective if initiated within t seconds following holding at beginning of shock; no delay if not holding.

cedure, the upper line records the presence or absence of the shock. When the shock is on, this line is displaced upward; when the shock is off, the line is down. The lower line records the position of the bar. When the bar is up, i.e., in its resting position, the line is up; when the bar is pressed, the line goes down and remains down for the duration of the hold. In each of the procedures, the rat is assumed to be holding the bar when the shock begins. The first diagram illustrates our original press procedure, in which the rat is required first to release the bar, if holding, then to press it to terminate the shock. The second diagram illustrates our usual release procedure, here termed "press-release" to emphasize the fact that releasing the bar is not effective until a press has intervened. That is, the animal must first release the bar, then press it, and finally release it a second time before he can terminate the shock. Three successive actions are required if the animal is holding when the shock begins. By contrast, only one action is required under the "immediate-release" procedure illustrated in the third diagram. The first release is effective. This is the new procedure added in the present experiment to amplify the advantage to be gained by holding the bar prior to the onset of the shock. Note, however, that the two release procedures are otherwise identical. In both cases, if the rat is not holding when the shock appears he must get the bar down before he can release it, and in both cases his position when the shock terminates is the same.

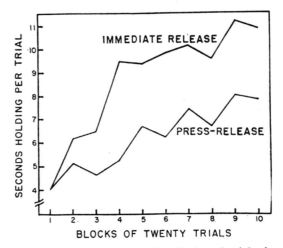

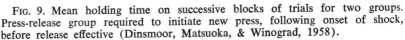

FIG. 9. Mean holding time on successive blocks of trials for two groups. Press-release group required to initiate new press, following onset of shock, before release effective (Dinsmoor, Matsuoka, & Winograd, 1958).

The results of these two procedures are compared in Figure 9. As was predicted, the mean time spent holding the bar increased more rapidly and reached a higher level for the immediate release animals than for those subjected to the usual press-release procedure.

The immediate-release procedure was also employed, independently, in a subsequent study by Migler (1963). Like our immediate release animals, his rats also showed an extremely high level of holding. Migler's data also confirmed and extended Campbell's findings by showing that these rats, too, terminated the shock more quickly when they were on the bar at its onset than when they were off it. His data for another group of rats subjected to the press procedure differed from those obtained by Campbell but were nonetheless consistent with our general analysis. Perhaps because of some difference in physical arrangements, his press rats took more time, rather than less, to terminate the shock when they had been holding. In other words, for these rats holding was not an effective preparatory response. As would therefore be predicted from our analysis of the source of the reinforcement for this form of behavior, these animals showed a decline in the amount of holding with continued training. Migler's interpretation of holding was essentially the same as our own.

In the second experiment reported by Dinsmoor, Matsuoka, and Winograd (1958) we employed another form of manipulation, more direct than before, of the temporal relationship between holding and the termination of shock. One of the groups in this experiment was trained in the usual way (press-release procedure), to provide a basis of comparison for the behavior of the remaining animals. Members of this group were required merely to release the bar, if holding when the shock began, and then press and release again. They were free to use their position on the bar as a preparatory response to permit more rapid termination of the shock. Members of the second group were free to terminate the shock as rapidly as possible if they were not on the bar when it arrived. But if they were on the bar, a delay of 1½ seconds was imposed. During this delay, pressing was ineffective: another depression and release of the bar were required after the 1½ seconds were up. This procedure was diagrammed in Figure 8, under the heading of "delay procedure." To put it simply, these animals were penalized for holding; following a hold, it always took them at least 1½ seconds to terminate the shock. Members of the third group were subjected to the same type of penalty, but in this case a delay of 3 seconds was imposed.

Again the results were consistent with our analysis. As may be seen in Figure 10, the mean number of seconds spent holding was greatest for the 0 delay group, less for the 1½ second group, and least for the 3 second group.

Two cautionary notes may, however, be appropriate. First, despite both the use of a release requirement for termination of the shock and the application of a substantial penalty for holding, the animals in our 3 second group still spent more than a fifth of their time holding the bar. The persistence of this form of behavior suggests that there may be other sources of strength that we have not considered. Secondly, the present explanation of holding suggests that it should be possible to develop the same form of behavior by using food or water to reinforce the first re-

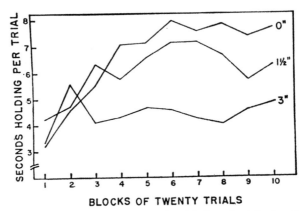

Fig. 10. Mean holding time on successive blocks of trials for three groups. Delays of 0, 1½, or 3 seconds imposed if animal on bar when shock began (Dinsmoor, Matsuoka, & Winograd, 1958).

sponse following the onset of a discriminative stimulus. Skinner (1950) has reported the development of functionally equivalent "waiting behavior" in the pigeon, but whether the rat would learn the specific response of holding the bar under comparable contingencies has not, to my knowledge, been determined.

A final implication of our analysis is that holding should be relatively ineffective under schedules in which the first response does not terminate the shock. If a number of responses are required, as in ratio schedules, preparatory behavior should have less effect, proportionately, on the length of time the shock remains on, and any such effect should be delayed for some time following the relevant behavior. The same would be true for interval schedules. Under these conditions, relatively little holding should be observed. The data have been consistent with this analysis, both for variable-interval (Dinsmoor & Winograd, 1958) and for fixed-ratio (Winograd, 1965) schedules.

ADAPTATION

Another problem that concerned us when we began our work on escape conditioning was that our subjects might "adapt" to the stimulus; that is, that their rate of response might decline substantially within each session as a function of the amount of exposure, leading to difficulty in evaluating the effects of other variables. While it is true that similar problems are encountered with other forms of stimulation—the subject is said to "satiate" with repeated presentation of food or water—it would be desirable to know the extent and time course of any such phenomenon.

The literature on adaptation to shock is not easy to evaluate. Most of the findings have been incidental to other data. Using human subjects, Seward and Seward (1934), MacDonald (1946), and Schneider and Baker (1958) have reported decrements in such measures as skin conductance, amplitude of breathing, general bodily movements, and verbal reports of painfulness or unpleasantness following repeated exposure. These measures, however, can be influenced by more general reactions to the situation. Using the techniques prescribed by Jacobson, Miller (1926) trained her subjects in relaxation. She found that the effect "was to reduce the extent of the movement, increase its reaction time, and diminish the apparent intensity or unpleasantness of the stimulus" (p. 41). The human subject, of course, is not truly naïve with respect to shock. MacDonald, for example, found a large change in skin conductance to the purely verbal stimulus, "Now you are going to get a series of shocks." This suggests that through some process operating in their natural environment her subjects had already learned an emotional reaction to the threat of shock before they entered the laboratory. But this reaction was disproportionate to the realities of the situation: after they had been exposed to a number of shocks, the changes in skin conductance to the same statement were much smaller.

Similar effects may be obtained with animal subjects. Using dogs, Kellogg (1941) found it necessary to increase the voltage used on successive sessions to maintain a leg flexion of constant amplitude. He attributed this effect to "a calming down of the subject, a decrease in general activity and in muscular tension, and an accompanying reduction in sensitivity as he becomes habituated to the experimental situation" (p. 95). He also found it necessary to use a higher than normal voltage at the beginning of each session, which he attributed to changes in the subject's resistance. But Schoeffler (1953), using a constant current stimulator, found that the amplitude and duration of leg flexion decreased with successive presentations. Overmier and Seligman (1967) found that a large percentage of their dogs failed to jump a hurdle in response to shock if they had been exposed to the same stimulus, while under restraint, the day before. If the exposure had been two, three, or six days earlier, however, their performance did not seem to have suffered.

The data for unconditioned responses by rats appear to be contradictory. Initially, Kimble (1955) found that jumping responses were less frequent during the second half of a series of 160 shocks. This is consistent with my own observations of a decrease in a variety of unconditioned responses to shock during much longer periods of exposure. But Trabasso and Thompson (1962) were unable to confirm this aspect of Kimble's data under almost identical conditions. Similarly, Hoffman, Fleshler, and Abplanalp (1964) found no change on successive sessions in the frequency or amplitude of the overall startle reaction, as recorded by movements of the animal's cage. Littman, Stevens, and Whittier (1964), on the other hand, found no change in the threshold intensity for squealing as a result of prior exposure but did find that a higher current was necessary to produce movements of the feet.

Generally speaking, the data obtained for rate of responding in free operant experiments do not indicate a uniform effect such as would be expected if changes occurred in the subject's sensitivity as a function of his exposure to shock. It is true that when mild shock is delivered as a punishment, pigeons may show a substantial recovery following the initial suppression of their rate of pecking (Azrin, 1960). Similarly, Hake, Azrin, and Oxford (1967), working with squirrel monkeys, found that with relatively low intensities of punishment the suppression of responding was more severe at the beginning of each session, followed by a gradual recovery. But Appel (1963) was unable to replicate Azrin's results with rats, even at the lowest intensities of shock.

While the "warm-up" effect obtained both with continuous and with discriminated avoidance procedures (e.g., Sidman, 1953; Hoffman, Fleshler, & Chorny, 1961) may be related to that obtained by Hake, *et al.*, it is opposite in direction to the effect that would be expected on the basis of a decreasing sensitivity to the stimulus. The rate of responding is often low at the beginning of the session, followed by a gradual acceleration to a stable level. In our own work, the same effect was frequently observed (although not always reported) when rate of responding was available as a measure of the animal's performance (Dinsmoor & Winograd, 1958; Dinsmoor & Clayton, 1963, 1966). It was particularly regular and prominent when the stimulus to be eliminated consisted either of a series of individual shocks, temporally separated, or a neutral stimulus accompanied by shocks (Dinsmoor, 1959, 1962). The form which it takes under these conditions, when the stimulus can be terminated for 60 seconds on a variable-interval schedule, is illustrated in Figure 11. Each of the cumulative records represents a 10-hour ses-

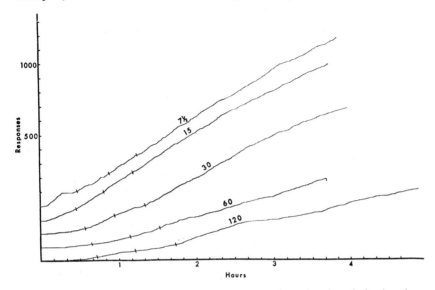

Fig. 11. Cumulative records of pressing that terminated series of shock pulses on a variable-interval schedule. Numbers indicate mean number of seconds between shocks (Dinsmoor, 1962).

sion for the same rat. The numbers along the baseline represent the cumulative length of time for which the animal has actually been exposed to the stimulus. The numbers next to the individual records indicate the mean length of the interval in seconds between successive shocks. In the top curve, the shocks are delivered, on the average, every 7½ seconds. The following curves are for 15, 30, 60, and 120 seconds. As can be seen by comparing the successive curves, the length of the exposure required for this "warm-up" to occur is related to the length of the interval between the shocks. The more frequently the shocks are delivered, the more quickly the animal begins to respond.

The same relationship is shown in precise, quantitative form in Table

TABLE 4: Mean Time Elapsed in Minutes Before First Response in Session (Dinsmoor, 1962)

Mean Seconds Between Shocks	Rat A No Signal	Signal	Rat B No Signal	Signal	Rat C No Signal	Signal
7.5	1.48	0.58	5.33	2.92	8.26	3.42
15	2.27	2.87	6.78	8.42	14.46	9.93
30	4.64	5.50	14.17	8.29	26.36	13.38
60	12.42	15.26	19.62	9.19	31.38	27.56
120	8.17	17.63	17.35	9.64	46.92	50.88

4. The measure presented in this table is the mean time in minutes before the animal makes his first response during the experimental session. Data are presented in successive columns for each of three subjects, both for the sessions on which a neutral stimulus or "signal" is presented, accompanied by shocks, and for sessions in which the shocks alone are presented without the stimulus. Looking down any one of these columns, you will see that the time required to make the first response increases with the mean interval between shocks, from 7½ seconds at the top to 120 seconds at the bottom. Under some conditions, the mean delay runs to 40 or 50 minutes. The source of this "warm-up" effect is not as yet clear, but what is clear is that it is opposite in direction to any effect to be expected on the basis of a decrease in the animal's sensitivity to the shock.

As could be seen in Figures 4 and 5 of the present paper, the rate of escape responding, under a variable-interval schedule at least, is extremely sensitive to changes in the intensity of the shock. Another method, however, which may be equally valuable in assessing the rat's sensitivity to shock, is that devised by Weiss and Laties (1958). Using what they called a "fractional escape" or "titration" procedure, these investigators plotted what amounted to a continuous measure of the rat's aversion threshold throughout the session. Every 20 seconds the shock increased one step in intensity; each time the subject pressed the lever, however, it was reduced one step. The authors found that "the amount of current tolerated by the rats did not shift very much within a session, nor did it vary appreciably from session to session" (p. 1575).

It is hard to tell exactly what previous investigators have had in mind when they referred to the possibility of their subjects "adapting" to the shock. Although the word has frequently been used, it seems never to have been defined. In some cases, the author may have been thinking of sensory adaptation, based on localized changes in the free nerve endings that serve as the receptors for pain. This type of adaptation would presumably take the form of a decline in responsiveness during each period of stimulation, i.e., within each session. In other cases, the author may have been thinking of an emotional adaptation, presumably involving widespread visceral and somatic changes that would in turn affect the motor response. While changes of this type would presumably be most prominent during the initial period of exposure, they might continue for a number of sessions. So far, experiments using shock—and I have cited only the simplest and clearest tests—have not provided sufficiently consistent evidence to support the existence of either phenomenon, or indeed, of any decremental process that might occur as an inevitable and inherent consequence of the subject's exposure to shock.

On the other hand, the evidence is abundant that changes sometimes do occur in the subject's reaction to shock. In some cases, these may be characteristic of the particular class of responses employed. In others, they may represent experimental artifacts based on inadequate control of the stimulus or on unrecognized contingencies between the behavior of the subject and the onset, presence, or termination of the shock. The experimenter may be well advised to test for the presence of such effects within the context of his own particular experiment.

The point may be illustrated by a series of three experiments we conducted to test the effects of prior exposure on the training of rats to press a bar for termination of shock. These experiments were conducted shortly after our first work with shock, when the only information we had concerned the parametric conditions suitable for training our animals. At that time, we did not expect prior exposure to have any effect on the animals' behavior, since our initial data had shown quick and reliable conditioning. However, we felt that the possibility was of sufficient importance to justify an empirical test. The results came as something of a surprise.

The general procedure which we followed in each of these experiments was to expose half of our animals to shock for a period of time before beginning their training. The other half were placed in the box for the same period but were not subjected to shock until the training began. An incidental feature of the first experiment (Dinsmoor & Campbell, 1956a), which I will not analyze within the present context, is that half of the shocked animals and half of the non-shocked animals had a bar in the box, which they were free to press, but which produced no effect. The other half of each group did not receive the bar until training began. For present purposes, we may treat this distinction simply as two replications of the same basic experiment.

In Figure 12 I have plotted the mean cumulative number of escape responses for each group for each minute of training. The top two curves, labelled NN and BN, represent the performance of the animals that had received no shock prior to training. The lowest total for any of the 16 animals in these groups was 53 responses. The bottom two curves, labelled NS and BS, represent the performance of the shocked

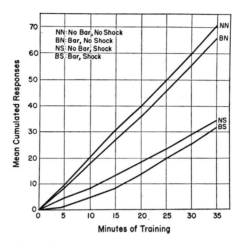

FIG. 12. Mean number of presses during escape training. Letters refer to
presence of bar (B) or no bar (N), shock (S) or no shock (N), during prior
exposure (Dinsmoor & Campbell, 1956a).

animals. Some of these made only a single response. The median number of presses was 24 for Group NS and 29.5 for Group BS. The difference was even larger than these figures would suggest, because the
animals that promptly turned the shock off as soon as it appeared spent
relatively little time in its presence, whereas the animals that failed to
turn it off spent a great deal of time in its presence. It is clear that
prior exposure to shock did interfere with subsequent training.

The next step may be difficult to follow but it is important to my
argument. On the next day, we returned our animals to the apparatus
for another period of exposure, just prior to extinction. During this
period, the bar was not present. Half of the animals in each of the
original groups were exposed to shock; the other half were not shocked.
Then the bar was introduced, and all animals were extinguished in the
presence of shock.

The results are presented in Figure 13. For present purposes, the
lower pair of curves, representing animals that were shocked before
the commencement of training, and the upper pair of curves, representing animals that were not shocked prior to training, can be treated
simply as replications of the same basic procedure for animals with different past histories. The animals that were shocked prior to training
(SN and SS), and consequently earned fewer reinforcements during
training, gave fewer responses than the animals that were not shocked

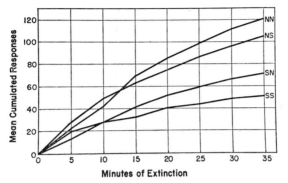

Fig. 13. Mean cumulative responding during extinction session in the presence of shock following escape training. The first letter for each plot indicates the presence of shock (S) or no shock (N) during pre-training exposure; the second letter indicates corresponding conditions during a period interpolated between training and extinction (Dinsmoor & Campbell, 1956a).

prior to training (NN and NS). But the difference to which I should like to direct your attention is the difference within each pair. In the lower pair, for example, the animals that had just previously been exposed to shock, labelled SS, responded more often during the first few minutes than their controls, labelled SN. I don't know whether this was a systematic effect or a matter of chance, but it was opposite in direction to the effect that would be predicted on the basis of a decrease in the animals' sensitivity to the shock. Later, in extinction, however, when pressing began to decline in strength, a delayed effect appeared: these animals pressed less often than their non-shocked controls. Similarly, in the upper pair the animals labelled NS responded more often during the first few minutes than those labelled NN, but responded less often during the latter part of extinction. Apparently the effects of prior exposure depend upon the current strength of the response at any given moment, and show up primarily at the beginning of training and at the end of extinction.

The model that we followed in interpreting these results was suggested by some earlier findings reported by Mowrer (1940). In that study, Mowrer first gave one group of rats a series of pretraining sessions in which they were exposed to a continuous, low voltage shock. All of these animals eventually learned to sit on their hind legs and hold their forepaws up in the air, away from the grid. This reduced the area of their contact with the grid. They were then trained to press a pedal, which turned the shock completely off, and were compared in their performance with a group of control animals that were being trained for the first time. The animals that had previously learned to sit on their hind legs were much slower at first in learning to press the pedal, but eventually learned to press as promptly as did their controls. The sitting response had at first interfered with pressing and had then in turn been suppressed by the pressing response, which was a more effective means of dealing with the shock. But later, when all the animals were punished rather than reinforced for pressing, those that had previously learned the sitting behavior abandoned pressing much sooner and reverted to their earlier form of behavior. In our experiment, the nature of the competing behavior was not as clear, but the same pattern was observed. The animals that had previously been exposed to shock responded at least as often as their controls during the early stages but declined more quickly as extinction progressed.

The main purpose of our second experiment (Dinsmoor & Campbell, 1956b) was to show that the effect we had obtained could not be attributed to sensory adaptation. In this experiment, we waited for 24 hours after the preliminary exposure to shock before we began the training. We argued that if our previous results had been due to changes in the receptor mechanisms for pain, the effect should dissipate within a reasonably brief period of time, well within the 24 hour limit; if, on the other hand, our results had been due to the learning of some form of competing behavior, this behavior should be retained during the period intervening between the two sessions.

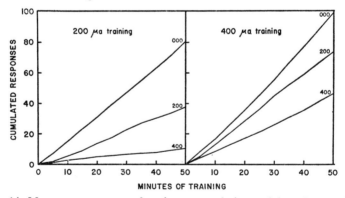

Fig. 14. Mean escape presses for six groups during training. Groups in the left panel trained at 200 microamperes, groups in the right panel at 400. Labels for individual plots indicate level of current to which group was exposed 24 hours earlier (Dinsmoor & Campbell, 1956b).

We also took advantage of this experiment as an opportunity to test the effects of different levels of shock on the phenomenon we were studying. During the preliminary period, one-third of our animals were exposed to no shock, one-third to a current of 200 microamperes, and one-third to a current of 400 microamperes. Also, half of the animals in each of these groups were trained with a current of 200 microamperes and half with 400. The results are displayed in the same form as before in Figure 14. The panel on the left shows the mean cumulative curves for the groups trained at 200 microamperes; the numbers next to each curve represent the level of current to which each group had been exposed twenty-four hours earlier. The panel on the right presents the same information for the groups trained at 400 microamperes. In both panels the curves representing different levels of prior exposure are well separated. It is clear that the effect did not dissipate during the 24 hours between the two experimental sessions. Therefore, it did not seem possible to attribute the effect to changes in the sensory receptors for shock.

The remaining problem was to identify the form of the competing behavior. This was not as easy in our experiment as it had been in Mowrer's. However, we had been watching our animals and had selected a possible candidate. The typical behavior observed during prolonged periods of non-pressing consisted of a sequence of rapid retractions of the forepaws from the grid, in rhythm with the pulsing of the shock, followed by somewhat slower replacements. This, we suspected, might have served to reduce the effective duration of each pulse. In reporting the results of our first experiment, we had suggested that by switching the polarity of the shock more rapidly for the different rods making up the grid, we might be able to complete the presentation and termination of an individual pulse before the animal had time to retract his paws. This form of behavior would no longer be as effective as before and would no longer compete as successfully with pressing. This hypothesis, then, was tested in the third experiment (Dinsmoor, 1958b).

For the third and final experiment in this series, I made use of the parametric information gathered in the second experiment. In that experiment, the largest effect had been obtained with the animals that were subjected to a current of 400 microamperes during their preliminary exposure but trained at a level of only 200 microamperes. Only two of the eight animals in that group had made more than a single response. This time, the same set of conditions was used, but the length of each successive pulse of shock was reduced from .113 to .048 seconds. Under these conditions, the previously shocked animals still did not match the performance of their non-shocked controls. But their improvement was impressive. In comparison with the previous median of 1.0 response for the session, they showed a median value of 72.5.

It is possible that some or all of the remaining difference between the previously shocked and non-shocked animals (median 113.5) can be attributed to the facilitative effects of such initial responses to shock as running, jumping, and rearing up on the hind legs (see Table 3); these responses were not recorded but appeared to decline in frequency as a function of continued exposure. It is also possible that other competing responses were learned, despite the change in the length of each pulse of shock. But the magnitude of the improvement suggests that we had correctly identified and removed a major component. The pre-exposure design seems to offer a sensitive method for testing the adequacy of various techniques for the delivery of shock.

Competing Responses on the Grid

The most convenient way to deliver shock to an animal is to place him on a grid composed of horizontal metal rods, each connected to the stimulator. The subject is then free to move about the box in the same way that he does in other studies using the free operant technique. Not only does this arrangement facilitate comparison of the resulting behavior with the data from other experiments, but its flexibility makes it relatively easy to duplicate the wide variety of relationships found in natural settings. As we have seen, however, the critical problem is to make sure that the stimulus is delivered according to the experimenter's specifications and is not altered in unintended and unspecified ways by the behavior of the subject.

The nature of the problem may be illustrated by the behavior that occurs when the successive rods making up the grid are simply connected in alternation to opposite ends of the shock stimulator. As is well known to most experimenters these days, this is a problem that is readily solved by the subject. When the animal stands on two rods that are attached to opposite terminals, he completes the circuit between these terminals, and the current flows through his body, as intended. But whenever he finds himself, by chance, on two rods connected to the same terminal, the circuit remains incomplete, and no current flows. The contingency faced by the subject is the same as that studied by such investigators as Hefferline (1950), Tolcott (1948), Winnick (1956), Harrison and Abelson (1959), and Leitenberg (1965). Movement away from this position to rods of opposite polarity is immediately punished by the receipt of the shock, and return to a safe pair of rods is immediately reinforced by its termination. It is also possible that this mode of adjustment is facilitated by a natural tendency for the animal to "freeze" in the position assumed at the moment when the shock was terminated. In any case, the animal soon learns to remain in a position where no shock is received.

Even when a switching circuit is used to shift the connection of each rod back and forth from one terminal to the other (Skinner & Campbell, 1947), additional problems are encountered. For one thing, it is necessary to electrify the lever and the walls of the box, which may make it difficult for the experimenter to watch the animal's behavior. With some switching circuits, certain pairs of rods may remain connected to the same terminal for a greater part of the time than others, and according to Sloane (1964) the animal may learn to reduce the temporal density of the shock by selecting and remaining on such a favorable pair. If the switching is too slow, the animal may reduce the duration of each pulse by placing his hind paws on one rod and lifting his forepaws from the other whenever the shock is encountered (Dinsmoor & Campbell, 1956a; Dinsmoor, 1958a).

When a high-voltage, constant-current circuit is used to present the shock, the current flowing through a given point (i.e., current density) decreases as a function of the area of contact between the subject and the electrode; the level of stimulation decreases in similar fashion (Jackson & Riess, 1934; Forbes & Bernstein, 1935). This means that an animal can probably minimize the effectiveness of the stimulus by gripping the individual rods making up the grid, provided they are sufficiently small in diameter to permit such a practice. And Mowrer and Miller (1942) have suggested that when the animal attempts to move across the grid he will probably be penalized by the incomplete contacts that result when he lifts and replaces his paws. Arcing between the subject and the grid may also discourage locomotion, unless an electronic shunt (Dinsmoor, 1960) is employed to suppress it. On the other hand, according to Mowrer (1940), when a low-voltage, variable-current stimulator is used, the animal reduces the total flow of current through his body by reducing the area of contact, i.e., by sitting on his hind legs and holding his forepaws in the air.

Moreover, with continued exposure, other forms of behavior may be discovered. Some animals, for example, learn to stand on their hind legs on a single rod, maintaining their balance by intermittent contact with the walls of the chamber. Others find that the shock is less effective if they lie on their back, interposing a layer of fur between their skin and the grid. Although this behavior can be reduced by removing the hair with clippers and depilatory compounds, it is not always possible to eliminate such avoidance behavior completely from the animal's repertoire.

One way of dealing with competing behavior is to limit oneself to procedures in which the shock is presented for relatively brief periods and the animal's time during these periods is largely occupied in performing the desired response. For example, as indicated earlier, when each depression of the bar serves to terminate the shock—continuous reinforcement—rats quickly and reliably learn to make this response, at least under the condition that we have employed. Migler (1963), moreover, has maintained rats on a continuous reinforcement escape procedure for as many as 24 one-hour sessions, without any reported difficulty. Similarly, Dinsmoor and Clayton (1966) found that rats readily learned to press when a variable ratio averaging three responses was required to terminate the shock. They were also able to maintain this pattern of behavior with conditioned reinforcement when the termination of the shock was delayed for 30 seconds after the last press. Winograd (1965) succeeded in maintaining behavior on fixed ratios as high as 20 responses, although he did report occasional "breaks" within the ratio runs at this value.

But the devil finds mischief for idle paws. While our first work with interval schedules (Dinsmoor & Winograd, 1958) yielded satisfactory intensity functions within each session, we did not attempt to maintain the behavior for a large number of sessions. Later, we conducted additional pilot work in which we used a multiple schedule with two components, one a variable-interval schedule of escape from continuous shock, the other a variable-interval schedule of escape from a stimulus accompanied by occasional pulses of shock. While the second of these procedures worked rather well when we attempted to match the corresponding rates of pressing, we found that under continuous shock our animals either responded at extremely high rates or not at all. The proportion of the session spent in pausing or in responding varied with the intensity of the shock employed, but intermediate rates seemed to be impossible to obtain. Although visual observation of these animals did not necessarily reveal any identifiable competing responses, the quantitative pattern suggested that relatively high rates of pressing were required to suppress alternative modes of action. When the rates dropped, other forms of behavior may have emerged that interfered with the pressing. We have also found in other pilot data that in many cases it is difficult to recondition bar-pressing once it has been extinguished in the presence of continuous shock. Limitations of this sort would certainly seem to restrict the usefulness of shock through a grid as a device for systematic study of aversively-maintained behavior.

Before we abandon all hope of using the grid for systematic work on escape behavior, however, I would like to offer one additional suggestion. I have just commented on the difficulty we had in maintaining intermediate rates of responding under a variable-interval schedule when continuous shock, broken only by the switching of the polarity of the individual rods, was used as the stimulus. But, as previously stated, the procedure involved two components, which were presented in alternation, in the form of a multiple schedule. After the rat had terminated the continuous shock, he was allowed a minute of relief, during which no stimulus was presented. The next stimulus was white noise accompanied by occasional, irregularly spaced pulses of shock. This, too, could be terminated on the same schedule as the continuous shock. The use of a multiple schedule provided a precise comparison between the behavior of the same subjects at corresponding points in their experimental histories under the two forms of stimulation. Under continuous shock, the behavior was extremely erratic, but under the noise it was usually quite satisfactory.

The orderly maintenance of behavior under a previously neutral stim-

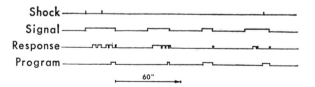

Fig. 15. Segment of polygraph record illustrating escape from conditioned aversive stimulus. Vertical displacements on successive lines show delivery of shock, presence of conditioned stimulus ("signal"), occurrence of response, and opportunity for termination (Dinsmoor, 1962).

ulus accompanied by pulses of shock came as no surprise. In earlier
work (Dinsmoor, 1959, 1962), I had conducted an extended study of
this type of performance, using a 500-cycle tone and a flashing light as
the stimulus. The experimental routine is illustrated by a segment of
the polygraph record reproduced as Figure 15. Time flows from left to
right, and the presence of the neutral stimulus (or "signal"), the shock,
or a depression of the bar is indicated at any moment by an upward
displacement of the corresponding line on the record. The experimental
sessions lasted for 10 hours, and each rat received more than a hundred
of these sessions. The work continued until two of the animals died,

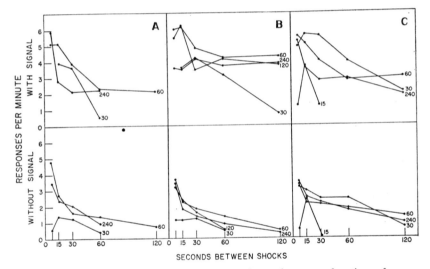

Fig. 16. Families of curves showing rate of pressing as a function of mean
interval between successive pulses of shock. A, B, and C are individual rats.
In upper panels, the presence or absence of potential shocks indicated by otherwise neutral stimuli (see Fig. 15). Numbers at the end of each plot indicate
duration in seconds of shock-free period produced on variable-interval schedule
(Dinsmoor, 1962).

presumably of natural causes; the third was then abandoned. The resulting families of curves for each of the three animals labelled A, B,
and C are shown in the upper part of Figure 16. The values represented
along the baseline indicate the mean length of the interval between successive pulses of shock, in the presence of the stimulus, and the values
distinguishing the separate curves represent the length of the time-out
following each termination of the stimulus. These values were varied

from session to session in an irregular sequence, in which the most important points were obtained early in the experiment and then replicated in later sessions in order to balance out any long-term changes in performance. Although the rate of responding dropped to less than one press per minute under some combinations of values, there seemed to be no difficulty in recovering appropriate rates in each case on the subsequent session.

Some control data presented in the lower part of the same figure were obtained during sessions that were intermingled among the sessions recorded in the upper part of the figure. The only difference between the control and experimental sessions is that the neutral stimulus or "signal" was omitted. Here, the typical rate of response is quite a bit lower, at least when the longer mean intervals are used between the successive shocks. This is natural, since at these values it is difficult to distinguish the interval between successive pulses from the shock-free or time-out period. The animal has no way of knowing, so to speak, when it is appropriate to respond, or, indeed, when he has ostensibly been reinforced by termination of the sequence. The surprise is not that the rat responds so infrequently but that he responds at all, and the mechanism involved may be more closely related to that involved in avoidance than to that ordinarily involved in escape.

It is important to note that satisfactory rates of responding are maintained during those control sessions in which the shocks are closely spaced, and that similar, although not identical, rates could be reproduced over and over again, on widely scattered sessions, throughout the course of the experiment. It is possible that the intervening "signal" sessions contributed in some way to the maintenance of this performance over such an extended period, and I did not attempt what might be considered the supreme test—extinction, with non-terminable shock, followed by reconditioning. Nevertheless, I think that the use of a series of discrete pulses of shock, with or without an accompanying stimulus, offers considerable promise for the free operant study of escape behavior. (See also D'Amato, Keller, & DiCara, 1964.)

ALTERNATIVE FORMS OF STIMULATION

In light of the difficulty that has been encountered in preventing the subject from developing competing responses to shock as an aversive stimulus, one might wish to consider the possibility of substituting some other form of stimulation, for use in the study of escape behavior. Bright light, loud noise, and low atmospheric temperature have each been offered as likely candidates. None of these stimuli have been widely used, and relatively little is known about their behavioral effects, but available observations suggest that each of them may have serious limitations.

Light has been used with some degree of success in several studies of bar-pressing in rats. However, its effectiveness for other species is open to question, and in the case of the rat it is known to have a depressive effect on the subject's level of activity (Skinner, 1958, pp. 254–257; Green, 1954). It is not clear to what extent this effect is due to light-reducing responses that, like the shock-alleviating responses on the grid, interfere with pressing (Hefferline, 1950, p. 266; Kaplan, 1952). The animal may learn to close his eyes, cover them with his paws or tail, use the shadow cast by the bar, or "bury" his head in a corner of the box. Conditioning appears to be more difficult than it is with shock. Often it is necessary to train the animal to press the bar by reinforcing a series of successive approximations to the final act (Kaplan, Jackson, & Sparer, 1965; Keller, 1966). In order to study the rate of pressing under fixed-interval schedules of reinforcement, Kaplan (1952) placed his animals on a specially designed "perch" designed to limit competing activities. Even with this precaution, however, he found that his rates reached their maximum values at an intensity of 183 milli-lamberts (25 w. bulb) and declined at higher levels. "Beyond a critical intensity," he suggested, "the depressant function . . . becomes increasingly predominant over the reinforcing effect" (p. 548). A similar maximum was also obtained in a later study (Kaplan, et al., 1965) in which the perch was no longer employed but in which every response in the presence of the light was immediately followed by a minute of darkness.

When noise is used as the stimulus, conditioning appears to be extremely slow and the final level of performance relatively low (Barry & Harrison, 1957; Harrison & Tracy, 1955). Campbell and Bloom (1965) compared the relative aversiveness of noise and shock across a range of intensities, using a tilt cage to record each animal's choice of stimulus. They found that their rats preferred exposure to the highest level of noise that could be used without risk of physiological damage (115 db) to exposure to an intermediate level of shock (55 volts AC through 150,000 ohms). They concluded that the ineffectiveness of noise "diminishes its usefulness as a motivating stimulus in psychological research" (p. 442). In some cases, it may have been possible for the subject to reduce the intensity of stimulation by changing the orientation of his head or his location within the experimental chamber. But even when a wire-mesh cage was used to restrict the animal to a relatively uniform sound field, the recorded behavior remained weak and erratic (Harrison & Abelson, 1959).

Low atmospheric temperature also appears to be limited in effectiveness. Weiss and Laties (1961), who have worked extensively with this form of stimulation, reported that rats deprived of their fur and exposed to a temperature of 2 degrees centigrade wait a mean of 5.16 hours before starting to press at a steady rate for bursts of heat. These authors suggested that "lever pressing must compete with other responses elicited by the cold, such as shivering and huddling. When shivering and huddling can no longer avert a further decline in (skin) temperature, they may then be replaced by gross motor activity" (p. 1343). This activity then leads to conditioning.

ATTACHED AND IMPLANTED ELECTRODES

It has long been recognized (e.g., Forbes, Muenzinger, & Wendt, 1935) that much better specification and control of the stimulus can be obtained with attached or implanted electrodes than with the grid. The problem is to find a suitable technique. In this section, I will review the solutions that have been offered for the three types of organism most commonly used in free operant studies—the pigeon, the rat, and the monkey.

In order to present shock to the pigeon, Hoffman (1960) has suggested wrapping a length of beaded chain around the base of the wing. We have made some use of this method in our laboratory, but have come to prefer a technique suggested by Azrin (1959). Although Azrin's technique calls for the implantation of two pieces of gold wire, it does not require surgical skills. In fact, it requires little beyond identification of the pubis bones and a modicum of courage. A short piece of gold wire is cut diagonally, to give it a sharp point, and thrust through the thin layer of tissue just above one of the bones. The ends of the loop are then brought together and crimped securely in the stem of a solder lug, together with a lead running to a miniature plug. The same operation is repeated on the other side of the bird. Finally, the plug is held in place with a leather harness (see Azrin, 1959). We have found that coiled, retractable cords, such as those used on telephones, provide suitable leads for connecting the pigeon to a telephone jack at the top of the box (Hoffman, 1960). This arrangement is excellent for suppressing positively reinforced behavior by delivering brief pulses of shock. However, pigeons have their peculiarities: no one, to my knowledge, has as yet successfully maintained the standard response of key pecking, at least, by reinforcing it with the termination or avoidance of shock.

I have been interested for quite a number of years in the possibility of implanting electrodes in rats. During this time, attempts have been reported to me in personal conversations with representatives of several different laboratories. How many other attempts have been made, unknown to me, is anybody's guess, but from the size of my personal sample I would suspect that the number must be rather large. In each of the cases that has come to my attention, simple logical considerations have dictated much the same technique. First, the leads from the shock stimulator must be brought in from above, so that they will not interfere with the animal's movements, and anchored to a relatively large portion of the skeletal structure. Some type of miniature plug is therefore screwed or cemented to the animal's skull, following the techniques that have been used for the presentation of intracranial stimulation. Secondly, the stimulating electrodes should be placed close to the surface of the skin, where pain receptors are available in plentiful supply, but in a region that is not readily reached by the animal's teeth or paws. Conductors are therefore led from the plug, underneath the surface of the skin, to some point in the animal's back, where the ends are stripped in order to make contact with the animal's tissue. Unfortunately, the effectiveness of this preparation for maintaining escape behavior has, to the best of my knowledge, never been given an extensive test. The reason is that in each case the electrodes have eventually either been displaced by the animal's activities or rejected by his tissues. It is possible that appropriate techniques will in time be found to meet this problem, but the disappointments have been numerous.

Another tempting line of attack for providing a more satisfactory delivery of shock to the rat is to apply external electrodes to the surface of the skin. The most obvious method is to use some kind of strap or harness to hold these in place. But the rat is a relatively small and agile animal, and where shock is concerned he becomes most determined. Weiss (1967) has recently used a tail electrode with some success, but most experimenters apparently have extinguished on such maneuvers and have turned to the use of some system of bodily restraint. Mechanisms for holding the rat in place have been described by Bijou (1942), Campbell (1959), Coppock (1950), and Hall, Clayton, and Mark (1966). Systems of restraint which are sufficiently severe to prevent the rat from escaping contact with the electrode are also likely, however, to exercise severe restriction on other activities and thereby to limit the flexibility of the experimental situation. A promising compromise which may prove to be useful in escape conditioning is the system developed by Azrin, Hopwood, and Powell (1967). The electrode is attached to the tail, as in other systems of restraint, but the restraining mechanism is confined to the same bodily locus. The animal cannot exert great pressure against this restraint, since the chamber is constructed with smooth walls that slope inward toward the locus of the restraint, affording no purchase for the animal's feet.

Earlier in this paper I mentioned the difficulty we encountered in maintaining escape behavior on a variable-interval schedule when we used rats on a grid. Suspecting that the inadequacies of the grid might be the source of our difficulty, we cast about for a more reliable method of delivering the shock. Our own attempts to implant electrodes were no more successful than those of others, and we felt that it would be easier to attach electrodes to a larger animal, like the squirrel monkey, than to the rat.

The first technique that we adopted, with fair success, was that suggested by Weiss and Laties (1962), in which the monkey was placed in a restraining chair and electrodes were attached to the bottoms of the feet. However, we still felt somewhat uneasy concerning the possibility that the subject might be able to change the firmness and extent of his contact with the surface of the electrode by pushing or pulling with his leg or by twisting his feet. Accordingly, we transferred our electrodes to a portion of the anatomy that is served by less adequate muscular control, the animal's tail. The technique that we have used for more than a hundred sessions each on several monkeys is that originally suggested by Hake and Azrin (1963). The tail is shaved at the appropriate places, rubbed with EKG Sol electrode paste, laid in a non-conductive trough, and overlaid with two hinged metal strips, which serve as the electrodes.

It may be helpful at this point to offer a few words of explanation, both to indicate the rationale for our work with monkeys and to illustrate the need for an adequate technology for maintaining behavior based on continuous shock. Many experimental psychologists believe that a stimulus that has repeatedly preceded the delivery of shock produces in the subject a reaction that is analogous to clinically-manifested and clinically-defined anxiety. Empirically, what has been shown is that the subject will learn, with fair reliability, to perform an arbitrarily designated response that terminates this warning signal and avoids the forthcoming shock. Furthermore, it has been found that a number of drugs that appear to be useful in treating human behavioral disorders are also effective in reducing the frequency of such a response (avoidance) in the animal subject; the same dose levels have little or no effect on responses that terminate the shock itself, once it has been delivered (escape). Portions of the literature on this topic have been reviewed by Herz (1959), Dews and Morse (1961), and Cook and Catania (1964). A tempting, though frequently questioned, interpretation of this phenomenon is that these drugs, particularly chlorpromazine, exercise a selective effect upon the animal's level of anxiety, and hence upon the behavior reinforced by its termination. Unfortunately, these findings have been based on techniques which I consider open to question, since they provide no control for other differences between the two procedures. First, the relationships between the avoidance response, the warning signal, and the shock are relatively complex; the contingency, or schedule of re-

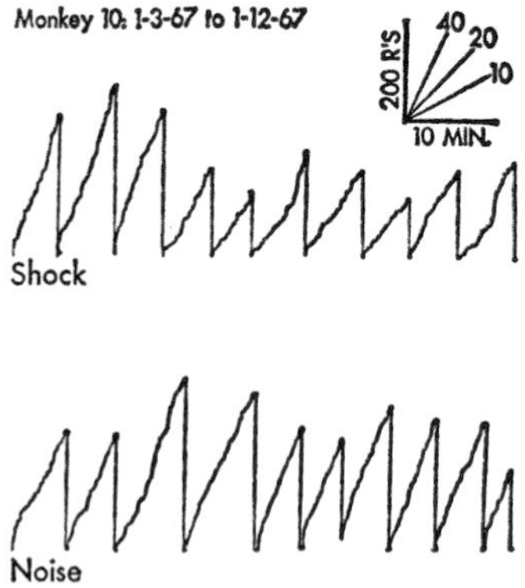

FIG. 17. Cumulative records for ten successive sessions of lever pressing maintained by termination of stimulus on variable-interval schedule. Upper set: continuous shock through tail electrodes. Lower set: white noise accompanied by occasional shocks.

inforcement, for avoidance appears to be quite different than that for escape. Secondly, even when the two responses are the same in form, the one that terminates the signal may be much more weakly maintained, and hence far more sensitive to any disruptive agent, than the one that terminates the shock. A wide variety of pharmacological compounds have been shown to have some differential effect on these two categories of response.

In our study of this problem (Dinsmoor & Bonbright, 1966), we attempted to provide a more precisely controlled comparison between the behavior maintained by the warning signal—consisting of a white noise accompanied by occasional pulses of shock—and the behavior maintained directly by continuous, but milder, shock. The two stimuli were presented in alternation, and each was terminated on the same variable-interval schedule by performing the same response, namely, pressing the lever. Finally, the rates of responding in the presence of these two stimuli could roughly be matched by raising or lowering the intensity of the shock. The resulting pattern of behavior is illustrated in Figure 17 by cumulative records obtained for 10 successive daily sessions, late in training, during which no drug was administered. The upper set of records shows the behavior in the presence of the shock, the lower set the behavior in the presence of the noise. It will be noted that in both cases the rate of responding remains at approximately the same level throughout the session and from one session to the next, despite a moderate downward drift in the presence of the shock. In other words, the behavior we have obtained seems to be comparable in its stability to that obtained when food or water is used as the reinforcer.

To demonstrate how the experiment came out, I will present a sample

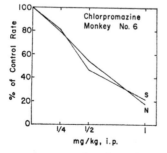

Fig. 18. Rate of lever pressing as a function of dose of chlorpromazine. S: escape from continuous shock. N: escape from white noise accompanied by occasional pulses of shock (Dinsmoor & Bonbright, 1966).

of the data for one animal, showing the effects of the drug. Figure 18 shows the rates of responding under three dose levels of chlorpromazine, expressed in each case as a percentage of the rate for the previous session. It will be noted that these three doses cover the effective range from relatively little to relatively complete suppression, and that at each level the effect is about the same for either stimulus. A more precise comparison is presented in Figure 19, in which the effect of each admin-

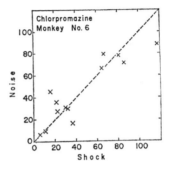

Fig. 19. Relative effects of chlorpromazine on lever pressing maintained by termination of continuous shock (horizontal axis) and by termination of white noise accompanied by shock (vertical axis). Each cross represents the respective percentages of control rates for a single session, and diagonal line represents the equality function (Dinsmoor & Bonbright, 1966).

istration of the drug is plotted on two coordinates. The vertical coordinate represents the relative rate of responding in the presence of the noise, the horizontal coordinate that in the presence of the shock. The diagonal line represents the set of points at which the two effects are exactly equal. Points below and to the right of this line represent instances in which the suppressive effects of the drug are greater on the behavior maintained by the noise than on that maintained by the shock. And the points to the left and above the line represent instances in which the suppressive effects are greater on the behavior maintained by the shock than on that maintained by the noise. As can readily be seen, most of the determinations lie close to the diagonal line, and those that depart from this line are found as often on the one side as on the other. Our conclusion, based on these and similar data for the other animals, is that chlorpromazine has no selective effect upon behavior maintained by conditioned aversive stimulation when the schedule of reinforcement and the rate of responding are appropriately matched.

REFERENCES

Appel, J. B. Punishment and shock intensity. *Science,* 1963, **141,** 528–529.

Azrin, N. H. A technique for delivering shock to pigeons. *Journal of the Experimental Analysis of Behavior,* 1958, **2,** 161–163.

Azrin, N. H. Sequential effects of punishment. *Science,* 1960, **131,** 605–606. (Republished: T. Verhave, Ed., *The Experimental Analysis of Behavior.* New York: Appleton-Century-Crofts, 1966.)

Azrin, N. H., Holz, W. C., & Hake, D. F. Intermittent reinforcement by removal of a conditioned aversive stimulus. *Science,* 1962, **136,** 781–782.

Azrin, N. H., Holz, W. C., Hake, D. F., & Ayllon, T. Fixed-ratio escape reinforcement. *Journal of the Experimental Analysis of Behavior,* 1963, **6,** 449–456.

Azrin, N. H., Hopwood, J., & Powell, J. A rat chamber and electrode procedure for avoidance conditioning. *Journal of the Experimental Analysis of Behavior,* 1967, **10,** 291–298.

Barry, J. J., Jr., & Harrison, J. M. Relation between stimulus intensity and strength of escape responding. *Psychological Reports,* 1957, **3,** 3–8.

Bijou, S. W. The development of a conditioning methodology for studying experimental neurosis in the rat. *Journal of Comparative Psychology,* 1942, **34,** 91–106.

Campbell, B. A., & Bloom, J. M. Relative aversiveness of noise and shock. *Journal of Comparative and Physiological Psychology,* 1965, **60,** 440–442.

Campbell, S. L. Resistance to extinction as a function of number of shock-termination reinforcements. *Journal of Comparative and Physiological Psychology,* 1959, **52,** 754–759.

Campbell S. L. Holding and behavior sequences in shock-escape. *Journal of Comparative and Physiological Psychology,* 1962, **55,** 1047–1053.

Cook, L., & Catania, A. C. Effects of drugs on avoidance and escape behavior. *Federation Proceedings,* 1964, **23,** 818–835.

Coppock, H. W. An investigation of secondary reinforcing effect of a visual stimulus as a function of its temporal relation to shock termination. Unpublished doctoral dissertation, Indiana University, 1950.

D'Amato, M. R., Keller, D., & DiCara, L. Facilitation of discriminated avoidance learning by discontinuous shock. *Journal of Comparative and Physiological Psychology,* 1964, **58,** 344–349.

Dews, P. B., & Morse, W. H. Behavioral pharmacology. *Annual Review of Pharmacology,* 1961, **1,** 145–170.

Dinsmoor, J. A. Punishment: I. The avoidance hypothesis. *Psychological Review,* 1954, **61,** 34–46. (Republished: Bobbs-Merrill Reprint Series in the Social Sciences.)

Dinsmoor, J. A. Punishment: II. An interpretation of empirical findings. *Psychological Review,* 1955, **62,** 96–105.

Dinsmoor, J. A. A new shock grid for rats. *Journal of the Experimental Analysis of Behavior,* 1958, **1,** 182, 264. (a)

Dinsmoor, J. A. Pulse duration and food deprivation in escape-from-shock training. *Psychological Reports,* 1958, **3,** 531–534. (b).

Dinsmoor, J. A. Variable-interval escape from a series of shock pulses. *Journal of the Experimental Analysis of Behavior,* 1959, **2,** 254. (Abstract)

Dinsmoor, J. A. Arc suppression in shock circuits. *Journal of the Experimental Analysis of Behavior,* 1960, **3,** 15.

Dinsmoor, J. A. Variable-interval escape from stimuli accompanied by shocks. *Journal of the Experimental Analysis of Behavior,* 1962, **5,** 41–47.

Dinsmoor, J. A., & Bonbright, J. C. Jr. A controlled comparison of drug effects on escape from conditioned aversive stimulation and from continuous shock. Paper read at Eastern Psychological Association, New York, April, 1966.

Dinsmoor, J. A., & Campbell, S. L. Escape-from-shock training following exposure to inescapable shock. *Psychological Reports,* 1956, **2,** 43–49. (a)

Dinsmoor, J. A., & Campbell, S. L. Level of current and time between sessions as factors in "adaptation" to shock. *Psychological Reports,* 1956, **2,** 441–444. (b)

Dinsmoor, J. A., & Clayton, Marilyn H. Chaining and secondary reinforcement based on escape from shock. *Journal of the Experimental Analysis of Behavior,* 1963, **6,** 75–80.

Dinsmoor, J. A., & Clayton, Marilyn H. A conditioned reinforcer maintained by temporal association with the termination of shock. *Journal of the Experimental Analysis of Behavior,* 1966, **9,** 547–552.

Dinsmoor, J. A., & Hughes, H. L. Training rats to press a bar to turn off shock. *Journal of Comparative and Physiological Psychology,* 1956, **49,** 235–238. (Republished: T. Verhave, Ed., *The Experimental analysis of behavior.* New York: Appleton-Century-Crofts, 1966.)

Dinsmoor, J. A., Hughes, H. L., & Matsuoka, Yasuko. Escape-from-shock training in a free-response situation. *American Journal of Psychology,* 1958, **71,** 325–337.

Dinsmoor, J. A., Matsuoka, Yasuko, & Winograd, E. Bar-holding as a preparatory response in escape-from-shock training. *Journal of Comparative and Physiological Psychology,* 1958, **51,** 637–639.

Dinsmoor, J. A., & Winograd, E. Shock intensity in variable-interval escape schedules. *Journal of the Experimental Analysis of Behavior,* 1958, **1,** 145–148.

Forbes, T. W., & Bernstein, A. L. The standardization of sixty-cycle electric shock for practical use in psychological experimentation. *Journal of General Psychology,* 1935, **12,** 436–442.

Forbes, T. W., Muenzinger, K. F., & Wendt, G. R. Report of Round Tables on the use of electric shock. *Psychological Bulletin,* 1935, **22,** 185–196.

Green, E. J. An anchoring effect in the operant responding of rats. *American Journal of Psychology,* 1958, **51,** 637–639.

Hake, D. F., & Azrin, N. H. An apparatus for delivering pain shock to monkeys. *Journal of the Experimental Analysis of Behavior,* 1963, **6,** 297.

Hake, D. F., Azrin, N. H., & Oxford, Rebecca. The effects of punishment intensity on squirrel monkeys. *Journal of the Experimental Analysis of Behavior,* 1967, **10,** 95–107.

Hall, R. D., Cayton, R. J., & Mark, R. G. A device for the partial restraint of rates in operant conditioning studies. *Journal of the Experimental Analysis of Behavior,* 1966, **9,** 143–145.

Harrison, J. M., & Abelson, R. M. The maintenance of behavior by the termination and onset of intense noise. *Journal of the Experimental Analysis of Behavior,* 1959, **2,** 23–42.

Harrison, J. M., & Tracy, W. H. The use of auditory stimuli to maintain lever-pressing behavior. *Science,* 1955, **121,** 373–374.

Hefferline, R. F. An experimental study of avoidance. *Genetic Psychology Monographs,* 1950, **42,** 231–334.

Hendry, D. P., & Hendry, Louise S. Partial negative reinforcement: fixed-ratio escape. *Journal of the Experimental Analysis of Behavior,* 1963, **6,** 519–523.

Herz, A. Drugs and the conditioned avoidance response. In C. C. Pfeiffer & J. R. Smythies (Eds.), *International Review of Neurobiology,* Vol 2. New York: Academic Press, 1959.

Hoffman, H. S. A flexible connector for delivering shock to pigeons. *Journal of the Experimental Analysis of Behavior,* 1960, **3,** 330.

Hoffman, H. S., & Fleshler M. Aversive control with the pigeon. *Journal of the Experimental Analysis of Behavior,* 1959, **2,** 213–218.

Hoffman, H. S., Fleshler, M., & Abplanalp, P. L. Startle reaction to electrical shock in the rat. *Journal of Comparative and Physiological Psychology,* 1964, **58,** 132–139.

Hoffman, H. S., Fleshler, M., & Chorny, H. Discriminated bar-press avoidance. *Journal of the Experimental Analysis of Behavior,* 1961, **4,** 309–316.

Hughes, L. H. Delay of shock-escape reinforcement. Unpublished doctoral dissertation, Indiana University, 1959.

Jackson, T. A., & Riess, B. F. Electric shock with different size electrodes. *Journal of Genetic Psychology,* 1934, **45,** 262–266.

Kaplan, M. The effects of noxious stimulus intensity and duration during intermittent reinforcement of escape behavior. *Journal of Comparative and Physiological Psychology,* 1952, **45,** 538–549.

Kaplan, M., Jackson, B., & Sparer, R. Escape behavior under continuous reinforcement as a function of aversive light intensity. *Journal of the Experimental Analysis of Behavior,* 1965, **8,** 321–323.

Keller, F. S. Light aversion in the white rat. *Psychological Record,* 1941, **4,** 235–250.

Keller, J. V. Delayed escape from light by the albino rat. *Journal of the Experimental Analysis of Behavior,* 1966, **9,** 655–658.

Kellogg, W. N. Electric shock as a motivating stimulus in conditioning experiments. *Journal of General Psychology,* 1941, **25,** 85–96.

Kimble, G. A. Shock intensity and avoidance learning. *Journal of Comparative and Physiological Psychology,* 1955, **48,** 281–284.

Leitenberg, H. Response initiation and response termination: analysis of effects of punishment and escape contingencies. *Psychological Reports,* 1965, **16,** 569–575.

Littman, A., Stevens, D. A., & Whittier, J. L. Previous shock experience and response threshold to shock. *Canadian Journal of Psychology,* 1964, **18,** 93–100.

MacDonald, Annette. The effect of adaptation to the unconditioned stimulus upon the formation of conditioned avoidance responses. *Journal of Experimental Psychology,* 1946, **36,** 1–12.

Migler, B. Bar holding during escape conditioning. *Journal of the Experimental Analysis of Behavior,* 1963, **6,** 65–72.

Miller, Margaret. Changes in the response to electric shock produced by varying muscular conditions. *Journal of Experimental Psychology,* 1926, **9,** 26–44.

Morse, W. H., & Kelleher, R. T. Schedules using noxious stimuli. I. Multiple fixed-ratio and fixed-interval termination of schedule complexes. *Journal of the Experimental Analysis of Behavior,* 1966, **9,** 267–290.

Mowrer, O. H. An experimental analogue of "regression," with incidental observations on "reaction formation," *Journal of Abnormal and Social Psychology,* 1940, **35,** 56–87. (Republished: *Learning theory and personality dynamics.* New York: Ronald Press, 1950.)

Mowrer, O. H., & Miller, N. E. A multi-purpose learning-demonstration apparatus. *Journal of Experimental Psychology,* 1942, **31,** 163–170.

Overmier, J. B., & Seligman, M. E. P. Effects of inescapable shock upon subsequent escape and avoidance responding. *Journal of Comparative and Physiological Psychology,* 1967, **63,** 28–33.

Schneider, M., & Baker, Katherine E. The drive-level of different intensities of electric shock. *American Journal of Psychology,* 1958, **71,** 587–590.

Schoeffler, M. S. Decrement of leg withdrawal response in a dog as a function of shock duration. Unpublished master's thesis, Indiana University, 1953.

Seward, J. P., & Seward, Georgene H. The effect of repetition on reactions to electric shock: with special reference to the menstrual cycle. *Archives of Psychology,* 1934, **27,** No. 168. (103 pp.)

Sidman, M. Two temporal parameters of the maintenance of avoidance behavior by the white rat. *Journal of Comparative and Physiological Psychology,* 1953, **46,** 253–261.

Skinner, B. F. *The behavior of organisms: an experimental analysis.* New York: Appelton-Century-Crofts, 1938.

Skinner, B. F. Are theories of learning necessary? *Psychological Review,* 1950, **57,** 193–216. (Republished: *Cumulative record.* New York: Appleton-Century-Crofts, 1959.)

Skinner, B. F., & Campbell, S. L. An automatic shocking-grid apparatus for continuous use. *Journal of Comparative and Physiological Psychology,* 1947, **40,** 305–307.

Sloane, H. Scramble patterns and escape learning. *Journal of the Experimental Analysis of Behavior,* 1964, **7,** 336.

Stavely, H. E., Jr. Effect of escape duration and shock intensity on the acquisition and extinction of an escape response. *Journal of Experimental Psychology,* 1966, **72,** 698–703.

Tolcott, M. A. Conflict: a study of some interactions between appetite and aversion in the white rat. *Genetic Psychology Monographs,* 1948, **38,** 83–142.

Trabasso, T. R., & Thompson, R. W. Supplementary report: Shock intensity and unconditioned responding in a shuttle box. *Journal of Experimental Psychology,* 1962, **63,** 215–216.

Weiss, B., & Laties, V. G. Fractional escape and avoidance on a titration schedule. *Science,* 1958, **128,** 1575–1576.

Weiss, B., & Laties, V. G. Titration behavior on various fractional escape programs. *Journal of the Experimental Analysis of Behavior,* 1959, **2,** 227–248.

Weiss, B., & Laties, V. G. Behavioral thermoregulation. *Science,* 1961, **133,** 1338–1344. (Republished: T. Verhave, Ed., *The experimental analysis of behavior.* New York: Appleton-Century-Crofts, 1966).

Weiss, B., & Laties, V. G. A foot electrode for monkeys. *Journal of the Experimental Analysis of Behavior,* 1962, **5,** 535–536.

Weiss, J. A tail electrode for unrestrained rats. *Journal of the Experimental Analysis of Behavior,* 1967, **10,** 85–86.

Winnick, Wilma A. Anxiety indicators in an avoidance response during conflict and nonconflict. *Journal of Comparative and Physiological Psychology,* 1956, **49,** 52–59.

Winograd, E. Escape behavior under different fixed ratios and shock intensities. *Journal of the Experimental Analysis of Behavior,* 1965, **8,** 117–124.

Use of Aversive Stimulation in Behavior Modification[1]

BRADLEY BUCHER AND O. IVAR LOVAAS[2]
University of California, Los Angles

SOME PRIOR CONSIDERATIONS

THIS REVIEW examines studies dealing with a special class of behavior modification techniques: those using aversive stimulation, such as electric shock or drug induced nauseous reactions, as a therapeutic tool. Aversive stimulation is uncommon in psychotherapy, and its use raises issues of both an ethical and experimental nature. We will briefly present our viewpoint on these questions here.

The experimental literature indicates two major problems that may result when aversive stimulation is used. One is based on data concerning its effectiveness, and the other on its unpredictable and often undesirable side effects.

The first problem, less frequently raised now, derives from early experimentation and theorizing tending to the conclusion that use of aversive stimulation was ineffective in producing permanent changes in behavior, and that the original behavior could confidently be expected to

1. The preparation of this manuscript was facilitated by Grant No. MH-1140 from the National Institute of Health.

2. James Q. Simmons, M.D., Chief, and Kathy Burnett, R.N., M.S. have collaborated in the work with noxious stimulation on schizophrenic children at the Neuropsychiatric Institute, U.C.L.A. Thomas Ball, Ph.D., Chief Psychologist at Pacific State Hospital in Pamona, and Lawrence Dameron, Ph.D., Fairview State Hospital, Costa Mesa, California were largely responsible for the research with Marilyn. We express our appreciation for the help of the staff at the Neuropsychiatric Institute and at Pacific State Hospital.

reappear when stimulation was discontinued. More than ten years of extensive research may now be marshalled in refutation of this view (Solomon, 1964). Aversive stimulation, used in a variety of experimental circumstances, may produce dramatic, varied, and long-lasting changes in behavior.

The second experimental problem is more serious. It is a by-product of the power that aversive stimulation has been revealed to have as a tool for behavior change. The experimental literature shows numerous examples of reactions that were not those specifically expected or desired. Some of these are pain, frustration, increased aggressiveness, arousal, general and specific anxieties, somatic and physiological malfunctions, and development of various unexpected and often pathological operant behaviors. As observed in specific instances, the above description includes a long list of undesirable reactions that have been at various times attributed to the use of aversive stimulation. Some of these reactions are temporary (pain); others may be long lasting and even fatal (gastric ulcers). Investigators and therapists must clearly be alert to these possibilities in developing and applying specific procedures.

The principal therapeutic uses of aversive stimulation have been as reinforcement in the elimination or establishment of operant behaviors, and reinforcement for creation of classically conditioned aversive stimuli, or even conditioned positive reinforcers. For these purposes aversive stimulation has been shown to produce profound effects. The problem in specific usage is to produce a desired result while monitoring and controlling for undesirable reactions. Current theory and research does not yield complete understanding and control of this problem, but development of specific well-controlled techniques appears feasible, as the work to be presented indicates.

Ethical and social issues in the use of aversive stimulation present enormous complexities. We can only touch on two issues: one concerning research into therapeutic effects of such stimuli, and one concerning use in actual practice. The work reviewed here bridges both questions since its intent is generally both experimental and therapeutic. It also belongs to the larger body of research into all aspects of aversive stimulation on human behavior.

We consider that the ethical justification for research on aversive stimulation derives from its importance in human experience. Aversive control is a traditional and common form of human social persuasion.

Prevalent social practice among the Western European and American middle classes appears to favor indirect forms of aversive stimuli, such as verbal aggression or deprivation of affection rather than methods that involve actual pain, but even here, use of actually painful stimulation is common in child rearing. Psychologists, as scientists, can hardly be justified in neglecting such powerful and pervasive methods of behavior control as subjects of research, however much they may wish to limit their application.

Most of the problems treated by the techniques reviewed here have also been treated by non-aversive therapeutic techniques. In general the ease of application and success of these methods have not been satisfying, and more effective techniques are desirable. If aversion therapy could be readily replaced with other methods, or if the problems treated were of little concern, ethical considerations might weigh against use of a procedure that cannot but cause some unpleasantness to the patient; however, such alternative possibilities do not now appear to be available. Of course, in specific cases the question of the appropriate treatment must always involve weighing such considerations.

Cautions issued by traditional therapists against the therapeutic uses of aversive stimulation have frequently been based on theoretical arguments quite unrelated to the learning principles that generated the techniques discussed here. To answer all these arguments within the various theories from which they derive is perhaps not possible, and a plea for a properly empirical attitude should serve as well. Our attitude throughout, generally without specific comment, will be that the aversion therapies discussed offer examples, if often poor ones, of a class of methods with genuine therapeutic promise, for which no alternative need necessarily be assumed, a priori, to be a greater benefit to the patient.

SCOPE OF THE PAPER

The present review will concentrate on studies using a learning model to guide use of aversive stimulation. Some of the work with schizophrenic children at the University of California at Los Angeles will be reviewed in some detail. Much of this work has not been reported previously. It is part of an extensive research program with these children, various results of which have been previously published (Lovaas, 1967). The research method used, the study of the individual subject, allows various uses of aversive stimulation to be illustrated with detailed presentations of data and measurement techniques.

A variety of other studies using aversive stimulation also will be examined. The patients involved are mostly nonpsychotics. Problems treated include principally enuresis, alcoholism, and various sexual deviations. Several procedures applied to these problems will be discussed critically, to elucidate the learning principles involved and the treatment variables responsible for the effects observed.

The use of behavior modification techniques with verbally proficient human beings presents a number of problems less pressing or not encountered with lower organisms and with nonverbal schizophrenic children. Some of these factors that we wish to emphasize include: the great variability in patients' environments and behavior outside the treatment room; the problems of control during treatment due to social interaction between patient and therapist; and the existence of verbal and symbolic events, often covert, in the patient's environment.

Therapeutic uses of aversive stimuli. There are several ways in which aversive stimulation can be used therapeutically. First, it can be used as punishment; that is, it can be presented contingent upon certain undesirable behaviors, so as to suppress them. This is perhaps the most obvious use of aversive stimulation. Second, aversive stimulation can be removed or withheld contingent upon certain behaviors. That is, certain behaviors can be established and maintained because they terminate aversive stimulation or avoid it altogether. Escape and avoidance learning exemplify this. A third way in which aversive stimulation can be used is to build stimulus functions. One such use is as a reinforcer in a classical conditioning situation, to create conditioned aversive stimuli. This technique has been used extensively in treatment of alcoholism and in several studies dealing with sexual deviations. Another possibility is less well known and most intriguing. A stimulus which is associated with, or discriminative for, reduction in aversive stimuli may acquire positive reinforcing (rewarding) properties. That is, an organism will work to produce or obtain stimuli that have been associated with reduction of aversive stimulation. The action of such "relief" stimuli is analogous to that of stimuli whose positive reinforcement properties derive from primary positive reinforcers.

These aspects of the use of aversive stimuli can be illustrated by observations of parent-child relationships. The first two are obvious; a parent will punish his child to suppress specific behaviors and the child will learn to behave so as to escape or avoid punishment. The creation of "relief" stimuli occurs more subtly, but is still quite common. Such a situation is one in which a parent rescues his child from discomfort. In reinforcement theory terms, the parent becomes discriminative for the reduction or removal of negative reinforcers or noxious stimuli. During the first year of life many of the interactions a parent has with his child may be of this nature. An infant will fuss, cry, and give signs indicative of pain or distress many times during the day, whereupon most parents will pick him up and attempt to remove the discomfort. Such situations may contribute a basis for subsequent meaningful relationships between people; individuals are seen as important to each other if they have faced and worked through stressful experiences together. It may well be that much of a child's love for his parents develops in situations that pair parents with stress reductions. Later in life, the normal child turns to his parent when frightened or hurt by psychological problems, by threat of punishment from his peers, by fears of failure in school, and so on.

Conversely, the parent, emitting verbalized and other cues for anger and intent to punish that have been associated with punishment, becomes an aversive stimulus for the child, arousing classically conditioned responses such as fear or aversion, as well as various operant behaviors of escape and avoidance.

These various uses of aversive stimuli may be combined in a single experimental procedure. For example, when an aversive stimulus is presented, another stimulus, such as a picture, or an object, or social signs of disapproval such as "no" or a frown, may be paired with its onset. Or, when aversive stimuli are removed, they are removed in the presence of another object, or of social stimuli significant of love and affection, to establish positive reinforcing properties for these stimuli.

In using aversive stimuli one faces, in selecting from these techniques, the choice of dealing directly with behavior or attempting to manipulate the stimulus functions in the environment that maintain those behaviors. It seems likely that the most valuable therapeutic use of aversive stimulation will not lie primarily in the suppression of specific responses or the shaping of behaviors through escape and avoidance training. Certainly, in the case of severely regressed psychotic individuals it would seem more efficient to use stress reduction as a way of establishing stimulus functions such as social reinforcers to help other people become meaningful and rewarding to that person. A treatment program centered on the establishment of a normal hierarchy of stimulus functions will give to the person's everyday social environment the tools with which that environment can build, and will modify the myriad behaviors necessary for a person to function effectively within it. In a sense, the person's behavioral changes would take care of themselves if he possessed a normal stimulus function hierarchy when moving from treatment to a normal environment. Such an approach is similar to more traditional treatments like psychotherapy, in which the therapist works with establishment or rearrangement of interpersonal meanings, rather than directly manipulating behavior.

The importance of establishing functions does not imply that the therapist can avoid dealing directly with behaviors at times. Certain behaviors have to be immediately terminated when these endanger the person's life, as in the case of self-mutilation in psychotic and retarded children. Similarly, certain intellectual behaviors are so complex that they can be acquired only in specific environments designed to create them. However, and particularly when one deals with severely regressed patients, and with pathological patterns of behavior that are maintained by a pathological environment, it seems virtually impossible to directly build all the behaviors the person needs to function adequately in society.

PUNISHMENT

We class as punishment those techniques in which the patient receives aversive stimulation after performing a response or response sequence that is an integral part of the behavior to be modified. Many of these studies include stimulus relations appropriate for the establishment of classical or respondent conditioning, so that whether the effect of treatment should be ascribed to response suppression by punishment or to the acquisition of aversion to specific stimuli may be unclear.

Schizophrenic children. Methodologically, the UCLA research with schizophrenic children can be described as follows: in almost all of the studies a single-subject replication design has been followed. This means that the independent variable, for example the aversive stimulation, is presented more than once (replicated presentations) to any one patient. Such a single-subject replication design seems ideal in clinical research since it allows for intensive observations of single individuals over long periods of time. It is particularly appropriate when one studies aversive stimuli, since the effects of aversive stimuli often show considerable differences from one individual to another.

Once a phenomena has been isolated in one patient, it is replicated formally over two to four other patients. Replications are then done for several (6–12) other patients on an informal or working-clinical basis. If replication of the findings fails, that particular patient or instance is then studied formally. The number of patients involved in the formal replication is some function of how complex the operations are, as defined by how many dependent variables are kept track of at any one time, and by whether the particular relationships are expected on the basis of previous findings. For example, subsequent to pairing the word "no" with the onset of aversive stimulation, it may be observed as expected that this word has acquired suppressing properties. In view of the enormous classical conditioning literature that supports this finding, formal replication need be done on no more than two patients. On the other hand, more replications are done when related experimental literature is not available to support the findings, as for example in studying the effect of noncontingent aversive stimulation on spontaneous behavior.

This research procedure is difficult to use with traditional hypothesis testing control group research methods, which usually require the application of a preset experimental design. In investigating the properties of aversive stimuli it has been difficult to formally plan out an investigation and then to gather patients for replication. The use of aversive stimuli, in any one case, is made contingent upon a clinical decision involving several professional people. Use of aversive stimulation is often a "last resort" strategy, and only on the basis of extensive familiarity with the child can the therapist rule out the effectiveness of alternate, more humane, interventions. In many cases, then, the opportunity to replicate across patients is a matter of chance.

A decision to use a particular form of aversive stimulation usually is made after trying out various forms on the particular patient. If a loud "no" proves ineffective, the next stimulus tried may be a painful slap on the child's buttocks, following which electric shock may be used if these preceding methods fail. The electric shock gives 1,400 volts at 50,000 ohms resistance, and is usually delivered by a hand-held inductorium.

Whenever possible, a number of behaviors is recorded, in addition to the one specifically selected for modification, to detect possible generalized effects on behavior. Sometimes it is these generalized changes that will determine whether aversive stimulation should be employed or not. In particular, changes may be recorded in generalized interpersonal behavior, such as bodily approach to, and withdrawal from, the attending adults. Sometimes physical contact or eye-to-face contact may be used to assess behavior in this dimension. Instances of changes in emotional behavior, such as fussing and whining, may be recorded, and the degree to which a child is withdrawing or psychotic may be assessed by measuring such behaviors as self-stimulation or echolalic and bizarre speech productions. These recordings are made on a button panel, where each button corresponds to a particular behavior and is wired into a multiple tape punch or Esterline Angus pen unit (Lovaas, Freitag, Gold, & Kassorla, 1965b). Since the recording apparatus is only semiportable, it has been impossible to record changes in response classes in situations outside the laboratory, such as the child's home.

Most authors using aversion therapy have indicated alertness to the appearance of undesirable (or desirable) side-effects. Concern for the generalized behavior changes with use of aversive stimulation derives both from their frequent appearance in the learning literature, and from the clinician's traditional fear for the development of substitute symptoms following "symptomatic" treatments. This concern is another consideration that points up the value of a research procedure that concentrates on the special factors in each individual case.

The work at UCLA is concentrated on the most severely psychotic children. They have been variously diagnosed as schizophrenic, autistic, retarded, and brain damaged; they will be referred to here as schizophrenic since they have been given that label most often. In general, the more diagnostic work-ups available per child, the more varied the diagnosis is likely to be. Instead of attending to the differential diagnosis, it is preferable to give a relatively detailed description of the particular behavior that is to be modified. Some children have been completely unresponsive to social stimuli and evidenced no social or intellectual behavior. Some have been so oblivious to their surroundings that they behaved as if they were blind and deaf. They were completely engrossed in self-stimulatory behaviors, such as spinning objects, rocking in sitting or standing positions, twirling, flapping their wrists, and gazing at lights and at their cupped hands. In some children vocal behaviors were limited to occasional vowel productions having no discernible communicative intent; at no time did the speech behavior of any one of these children even approximate adequacy, being restricted to echolalic-like productions with an understanding of only the most primitive commands. The majority of the children evidenced no appropriate play behavior. About 75% of the children would engage in tantrum behaviors, which included smearing of feces, biting attending adults, and self-mutilation. Some of these children came from other treatment centers where they had been seen for extensive periods of time with no discernible improvements; others had been rejected from treatment because they were thought to be poor treatment risks. Some of these children have been studied in inpatient settings and others as outpatients. Some of the inpatients have been seen for a total of almost eight hours a day, five days a week, while others have been seen for only three to five hours a week on an outpatient basis.

Work using punishment with schizophrenic children has been primarily directed toward direct suppression of two kinds of pathological behaviors: self-stimulation and self-destruction. These will be discussed separately.

Self-destructive behavior has been present in the majority of the children in the UCLA project. The most common form of self-destruction appears to be head-banging; the child will hit his head against sharp corners of the furniture, the walls, and strike his face with his fists. Another form includes biting, usually of hands and shoulders. It is relatively rare to see schizophrenic children engage in other forms of self-destruction, although one occasionally sees a child who brings his knee to his head or kicks the wall with his feet. We have not observed children using objects such as knives to mutilate themselves.

Self-destructive behavior is a difficult clinical problem to control, and it is quite demoralizing to the staff, perhaps because such children obviously suffer and have to be tied down. As is true of many clinical problems, there were hardly any objective experimental data on the nature of self-destructive behavior. The few data available (Wolf, Risley, & Mees, 1964; Lovaas, Freitag, Gold, & Kassorla, 1965a) showed functional relationships between various specific environmental operations and self-destruction, which made it most reasonable to regard self-destructive behavior as learned, operant, or instrumental social behavior. Quite surprisingly, it appeared that sympathetic comments, given contingent upon the occurrence of self-destructive behavior (the treatment usually prescribed for such children) made the child worse. Similarly, the removal of such comments served to effectively extinguish the behavior.

Use of aversive stimuli to suppress self-destruction involves the ethical problems previously commented on. These problems were considered for the specific treatment setting at hand (state hospitals). The poorest alternative appeared to be to leave the child in continued restraints with concurrent curtailment of phychological growth and risk of severe physical damage. The question became one of which treatment procedure to employ. Using our knowledge of learning as a guide, there are these alternatives: extinction by reinforcement withdrawal, suppression by noxious stimuli, and the establishment of incompatible behavior. A previous study (Lovaas, *et al.*, 1965a) found that self-destructive behavior could be suppressed by building incompatible behaviors, and perhaps this would be the most humane and effective procedure. However, the children to be treated here came from hospitals where building incompatible behaviors was judged unfeasible. The wards were understaffed (a particular nurse having to deal with as many as 20 children), and were staffed by personnel unfamiliar with shaping. In fact, the failure of the ward environment to provide reinforcement for alternate behaviors may have created, maintained, and increased the self-destructive behavior. The viable alternatives, then, center on extinction versus suppression with aversive stimulation. Which to use should be some function of the extent to which the child would be exposed to suffering during treatment. The following case of John serves to illustrate this matter, and unequivocally points to the use of aversive stimulation as the more humane treatment for this situation.

John was a seven-year-old boy, diagnosed as retarded (IQ 25), with psychotic-like behaviors. He had been self-injurious since he was two years of age, a behavior which necessitated his hospitalization one year prior to his being studied at UCLA. During that year he had to be kept in complete restraints (legs, waist, and with a camisole to restrain his arms) on a 24-hour a day basis. When removed from restraint he would immediately hit his head against the crib, beat his head with his fists, and scream. He looked extremely frightened when removed from restraints. He was so unmanageable that he had to be fed in full restraints; he would not take food otherwise. His head was covered with scar tissue, and his ears were swollen and bleeding.

John was studied in several situations, and the two of particular in-

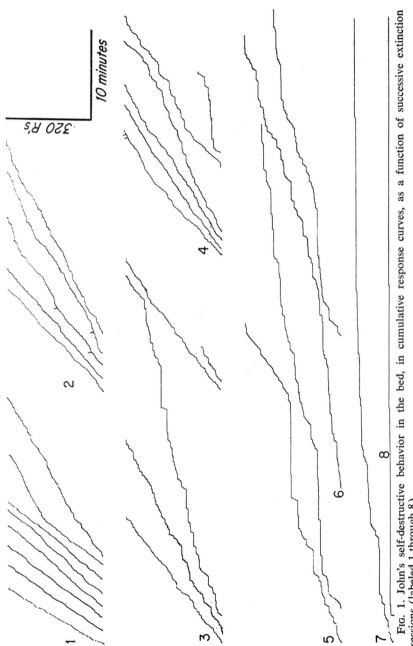

Fig. 1. John's self-destructive behavior in the bed, in cumulative response curves, as a function of successive extinction sessions (labeled 1 through 8).

terest here will be referred to as the extinction situation and the punishment situation. The extinction situation was carried out as follows: for
one and one-half hours every day, for eight days, John was simply left to
himself in his bed without restraints, with no attention given to his self-
destructive actions. The extinction record of his self-destruction is presented in Figure 1. Days are labeled 1 through 8. It can be observed
that rate fell very gradually from the first day, when it was as high as
approximately 3,000 self-injurious acts, in one and one-half hours, until
it reached a low of 15 acts on the eighth day. Although he eventually
did go to extinction or near extinction, he hit himself in excess of 10,000
times. Even though John was a "careful" hitter, the medical staff expressed considerable concern for damage caused by edema of his ears.
Extinction in the bed did not affect his self-destructive behavior in other
situations, such as the living room, as presented below.

John's extinction by the use of aversive stimuli (electric shock), given
contingent upon self-destructive behavior, is in marked contrast with
extinction data in Figure 1. The punishment data is presented in Figure
2. The first 15 sessions are pre-experimental, and show no trends either

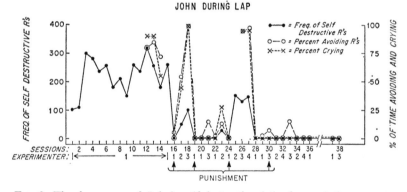

FIG. 2. The frequency of John's self-destructive behavior and the percentage
of crying and avoiding adults, in the living room, as a function of shock. The
ordinate gives sessions and the particular experimenter (attending adult) present
during these sessions. Shock was given by Experimenter 1 on sessions 16, 19 and
24, and by Experimenter 3 in session 30.

toward improvement or worsening. Punishment, in the form of 1-second
electric shocks, was introduced in session 16 with dramatic results. John
received a total of 12 shocks distributed over sessions 16, 19, 24 and 30.
There was a two-week time span between sessions 36 and 37, and it can

be observed that his rate was down, even without shock, during that time period. Two additional observations are of interest. The first pertains to generalization of suppression across situations. During the first 29 sessions he was only punished by Experimenter 1. The suppression effected by Experimenter 1 generalized only partly to Experimenters 2, 3, and 4. By sessions 25, 26 and 27, his rate was climbing alarmingly with other experimenters. However, when Experimenter 3 administered aversive stimuli on the 30th session the suppression effect generalized across experimenters.

The second observation of interest pertains to generalization of the treatment effect to quite different behaviors. As self-destructive behavior is brought down by shock, John avoided attending adults less and also cried less. Apparently, avoiding, crying, and self-destructive behavior fall within the same response class. So far as the behaviors recorded in this instance show, the side effects of shock are desirable. Informal clinical observations further confirm this finding (John was observed by some 20 staff members). Freedom from restraints permitted many reinforcing discoveries; he would run, scratch himself, play in the tub, and in general act more like a boy. However, there are no reasons why the side-effects of shock-produced suppression should always be desirable. (The side-effects probably should vary as a function of the particular child's reinforcement history.)

Linda received the same treatment as John for self-destructive behavior and showed almost identical changes. Linda was seven and one-half years old; she had been diagnosed as retarded, with an IQ of 33. She had been self-destructive since she was one and one-half years of age, and had been hospitalized for one and one-half years prior to being admitted to the UCLA project, having been in restraints for that entire period. Like John, she had a long history of treatment with drugs. Unlike John, who had been tied to his bed, Linda had moved about on the ward, but with her hands tied to her thighs in order to prevent her from beating her ears with her hands or shoulders. Her ears and head were covered with scar tissue; her ears were swollen and bleeding. She had developed cataracts during her hospitalization and was effectively blind.

The data on Linda's self-destructive behavior is shown in Figure 3. Two sessions were run every day. There were no systematic changes in her self-destructive behavior over the pre-experimental sessions (1 through 15). A total of 15 shocks were distributed over sessions 16, 17, 19 and 21. "No" was paired with shock in each of these sessions and

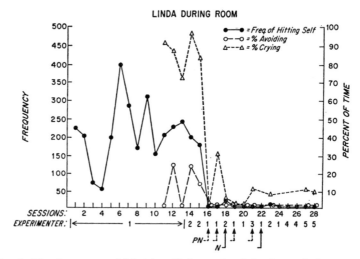

Fig. 3. The frequency of Linda's self-destructive behavior and the percentage of avoiding and crying, in the living room, as a function of shock. The ordinate gives sessions and the particular experimenter present during these sessions. Shock (P) and/or "no" (N) was administered by Experimenter 1 during sessions 16, 17, 19 and 22, by Experimenter 2 in session 18, and Experimenter 3 in session 21.

used without shock in sessions 18 and 23. It can be observed that shock brought self-destructive behavior immediately to zero and kept it there for the remainder of the study. As with John, generalized behavior change accompanying the shock showed up as a decrease in whining and fussing and a decrease in avoiding attending adults. She also discriminated between punishing and nonpunishing adults, as John had done.

Additional data on self-destruction supports the data on John and Linda. One of the most severe cases seen was *Marilyn*. She was a 16-year-old child diagnosed as retarded (moderate range) with psychotic features. She had been hospitalized for the previous two years, and had been self-injurious since she was two years old. The referring complaint centered on the parents' inability to control her self-destructive behavior. During her two years of hospitalization she had been kept in a camisole in an attempt to prevent this behavior. When removed from the camisole, or when she removed the camisole on her own by her teeth, she would bite her hands so severely that at one time her little finger on her right hand had to be amputated to the first joint. She would, similarly, with her teeth remove her nails by their roots. She was also a head-banger; her scalp was covered with scar tissue. She would fall to the ground without apparent reason, scream, and occasionally aggress toward others by biting them.

The first session lasted for about 2 hours; halfway into the session she was given shock for self-destructive behavior. The suppresion data on Marilyn is virtually identical to that of John and Linda. Her rate of "spontaneous" injury was very low, and in that way very different from John and Linda. Her self-destructive acts were highly discriminated: she would mutilate herself whenever the experimenter gave her affection, such as comforting her or praising her (33 self-injurious behaviors out of the 36 such interactions with her prior to shock). A total of 5 shocks (on the 1st, 4th, 5th and 15th presentation of the affectionate interaction) brought her biting and head-banging to zero, and it remained at zero level for the rest of the session.

Marilyn demonstrates well, because of the extreme severity of her self-injurious behavior, why it is impossible to place such a child on extinction. Marilyn could have inflicted serious self-injury or even killed herself during an extinction run.

While the immediate generalized behavior change due to shock was very favorable, and in that way similar to John and Linda, there is some reason to believe that her aggression toward other children on the ward increased at a later time. Apparently, the reinforcers which maintained the self-destructive behavior were still operative, and since she did not develop a more acceptable behavior form, which seems to be the case in most children (e.g., John and Linda), and was not explicitly trained to behave otherwise, she returned to a form of behavior which yielded large quantities of attention.

It is obvious that the durability of suppression will be a function of the "post-treatment" environment. The data we have illustrated in Figures 2 and 3 point to the extensive discriminations made by these children (among adults, physical settings, and so on). If the child returns to the ward that previously reinforced this behavior and if that environment remains unaltered, then it should only be a matter of days before the child has to be placed back into restraints.

The data given here on the suppression of self-injurious behavior by use of aversive stimulation are quite similar to those obtained by Risley (1967). Specifically, Risley punished an autistic girl with electric shock for climbing in high places (such as trees and houses), a behavior which threatened the child's life. Risley brought this behavior under very effective control and observed, as has been shown here, that the generalized effects of shock were not undesirable, in that shock was accompanied by an increase in the child's eye-to-face contact with attending adults. He found no change in the child's self-stimulatory or tantrum behavior (which had not been experimentally punished) as a function of shock. Hitzing and Risley (1967) report on a severely retarded child who had been restrained for several months to protect her from head-banging and biting. When punished (with slaps) for head-banging, that form of self-destruction was immediately suppressed, but biting remained at its pre-experimental level until it also was punished. Pre-punishment observations demonstrated the highly discriminated nature of the self-destructive behavior—the child's "spontaneous" rate being low, but rising immediately in the company of adults. The consistency of their observations with those presented here is apparent. Tate and Baroff (1966), Kushner (1967), and Hamilton[3] have reported similar reductions in the self-destructive behavior of retarded and psychotic children when painful electric shock is given contingent upon the behavior.

We turn now to work on suppression of self-stimulatory behavior. Self-stimulatory behavior is the most predominant form of pathological behavior seen in autistic children. In each case that we have seen where the primary diagnosis was autism, the children have engaged in self-stimulation. In some cases this behavior occupies 99% of their waking hours. Clinically, the children seem particularly unresponsive and inattentive to their external environment when engaged in this behavior, an observation which is gaining experimental confirmation in the UCLA laboratory. It was therefore judged appropriate, for educational and therapeutic purposes, to attempt to suppress this behavior.

Shock, contingent upon self-stimulatory and tantrum behaviors, was given to two schizophrenic children who were identical twins. They were five years old when the study was initiated and diagnosed as autistic. They evidenced no social responsiveness; they were mute, and did not play appropriately. They were greatly involved in self-stimulatory behavior, spending 70% to 80% of the day rocking, fondling themselves, and moving their hands and arms in repetitive stereotyped manners. Each child who engaged in self-stimulatory behavior was given shock

---

3. J. W. Hamilton, personal communication, 1967.

of 1-second duration. Whenever possible shock was administered at the onset of the behavior. The data on the suppression of self-stimulation is presented in Figure 4. The dates and treatments are presented on

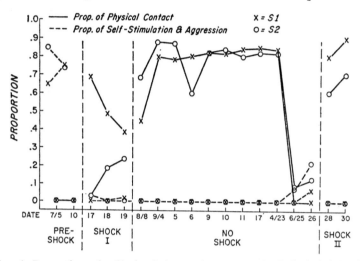

FIG. 4. Proportion of self-stimulation and tantrums (pathological behaviors) and physical contact (social behaviors) in twins, as a function of shock administration.

the abscissa. Prior to the delivery of shock, self-stimulatory and aggressive behavior varied between 65 and 85% for both of these children. During shock administration (shock 1) these behaviors fell immediately to zero, and remained at zero level for eleven months, after which there was a sudden increase in these behaviors. One noncontingent shock (during shock 2) immediately re-suppressed these behaviors. The concurrent increase in physical contact with the attending adults is partly (but not totally) a function of approach behavior built concurrently, and is discussed in the section on escape and avoidance learning.

These are the only two children who have been systematically studied for the effect of shock on self-stimulation. Another ten children have been seen in clinical contact, where aversive stimuli given contingent upon self-stimulatory behavior has a similar effect to that presented in Figure 4.

Treatment of nonpsychotic patients. We review here studies treating alcoholism, smoking, fetishism, transvestism, drug addiction, and compulsive sadistic fantasies. In most cases, the patients are either outpatients, or are hospitalized briefly. The environment in which the pathological behaviors occur is generally not, or not only, that of hospitals so that generalization of the effect of treatment to all relevant situations cannot be directly observed. Also, in most cases the pathological behaviors can be reproduced only approximately in the hospital settings, so that punishment for the behaviors likely to occur outside may not be possible. These factors complicate treatment and treatment evaluations, not only when punishment is used, but for other forms of aversive stimulation as well.

A typical example of a punishment procedure is that of Blake (1965), who treated alcoholics using shock as the punishing stimulus. Patients mixed a drink from a selection made available, and received shock after taking a sip. Spitting out the liquid terminated shock. Shock was given on only 50% of the trials; a light was the signal to the patient to spit out the liquor on the other trials. Whether punishment or classically conditioned aversion is more effective here is unclear. Blake does not indicate that the behavior changes observed in his patients were related in any way to the specific behavior sequence punished, and he did not label his procedure as punishment trials. Mixing of a drink is not a part of typical behavior of many drinkers, but may be relevant for others. The punished behavior sequence allows a variety of stimuli associated with drinking to be associated with shock, so that acquired aversion may be the principal effective agent of change. No specific data on this question were provided. Certainly some information on this question is desirable if, as in some cases here, the requirement for the patient to engage in a complex behavior sequence poses some experimental difficulties.

An interesting variation on the above procedure involves use of imaginal responses in a punishment technique. Kushner and Sandler (1966) report treatment of a patient with persistent suicidal thoughts. Shock was delivered contingent on a signal from the subject indicating that he had a clear image of a suicidal action. Such thoughts are quite possibly early components of a behavior that could lead to suicidal acting out. Kushner and Sandler also class as punishment a case in which the patient received shock for imagining an external object associated with fetishistic activity. We class this case as aversion conditioning, by analogy with a procedure in which the object would actually be presented to the patient just prior to shock.

The experimental economy of the above procedure is clear. Its effectiveness relative to a procedure using an overt behavior sequence has not been investigated. The use of imaginal events to model external situations is widely used in desensitization therapy, but is less common in studies using aversive stimulation.

Glynn and Harper (1961) and Morgenstern, Pearce and Rees, (1965) treated transvestites using apomorphine, administered every 2 hours. Apomorphine is an emetic that produces nausea and vomiting a few minutes after administration. Following the therapist's instructions, the patients dressed themselves in women's clothing during the nauseous reaction. Similarly, Raymond (1963) treated addictions using apomorphine. He required each patient to carry out a relevant behavior— drinking, smoking, or self-administering a drug—while nauseous. These studies report considerable success, but provide insufficient data to make possible a careful functional analysis of just what behavior changes were brought about, and how they were accomplished.

Use of apomorphine makes evaluation of treatment factors difficult because the drug effect is spread over a considerable period of time, and may involve several stages of rising and decreasing nausea and vomiting. Electric shock is clearly superior for control of intensity and timing.

Blakemore, Thorpe, Barker, Conway, & Lavin, (1963) used electric shock in a procedure that is quite similar to those using apomorphine, as just described. The patient, a transvestite, was instructed to dress in woman's clothing in a treatment room with a metal grid floor. Shock was given after dressing had continued for 1 to 3 minutes. At the first shock the patient began to undress, as previously instructed, and received occasional shocks while doing so. This procedure appears to combine punishment and escape. The dressing behavior punished appears relevant to the elimination of the cross-dressing behavior typical of transvestites, but the undressing, or escape, behavior does not, since it can begin only after some cross-dressing occurs. The justification for the use of this latter part of the procedure is unclear.

In a later review of this study, Blakemore (1964) was uncertain whether the behavior change achieved here should be attributed to classical or instrumental conditioning. If classical conditioning of aversion to the cues associated with the act of dressing and undressing is the effective factor, then the procedure is unnecessarily complex and cumbersome. A simpler procedure could have provided better control of the contingencies necessary for aversion conditioning to occur.

Blakemore *et al.* (1963) used a buzzer instead of shock on some trials. The first buzzer cued the patient to begin to undress, and further buzzer signals were given during the undressing, in conformity with the use of shock on shocked trials. The first buzzer thus provided a discriminative cue that shock would not be present during the trial. This appears to establish conditions for a discrimination for presence and absence of aversive stimulation—a procedure that, as has been seen, can lead to differential suppression.

Wilde (1964), and Franks, Fried, and Ashem (1966) used concentrated cigarette smoke as the aversive stimulus in attempting to eliminate cigarette smoking behavior. Patients received this stimulation continuously while smoking a cigarette. The smoke was blown from a specially-constructed machine in which several lighted cigarettes had been placed. Since this concentrated smoke is quite unpleasant, stimuli associated with smoking should become aversive. Further, since smoke, the aversive stimulation, is also associated with the act of smoking, cigarette smoke produced while smoking may become aversive by generalization from the concentrated smoke used as the aversive stimulus.

The problem of discrimination between treatment setting and the outside environment may be especially serious in this procedure. Patients were not required to stop smoking outside during the course of the experimental sessions. If repeated, unpunished smoking occurred outside at the same time that smoking was punished in the training setting, then this provided conditions suitable for discrimination training. Establishment of such a discrimination could be further facilitated by the large and salient smoke-blowing apparatus into which the patient was instructed to look during each trial. The apparatus cues may thus become part of the conditioned aversive stimulus.

Similar criticism applies to the Koenig and Masters (1965) procedure, in which patients were punished with shock on a 50% partial reinforcement schedule, at 18 discriminable steps during the course of smoking a cigarette. Patients were encouraged but not required to stop smoking during the period of treatment. No special provisions appear to have been made to minimize laboratory cues that may have become part of the conditioned aversive stimulus or facilitated discrimination training.

The problem of generalization of training from the laboratory to the outside environment is an important one for all the procedures so far examined. The discriminative cues controlling operants in the environment can seldom be exactly reproduced in a contrived setting. A reasonably normally functioning adult patient can verbally distinguish punished and unpunished situations on the basis of very minor cues, which may become salient as a result of this cue function. How behavioral reactions are affected by these intellectual discriminations is a problem for which little information is available. In the absence of more precise control, a wise procedure would appear to be to minimize the objective discrepancies between the treatment environment and the environment in which the pathological behavior normally occurs; and to eliminate as far as possible patient behaviors that may facilitate establishment of behavioral discriminations.

McGuire and Vallance (1964) used a punishment technique similar to that of Koenig and Masters, with ten smokers. These patients were not permitted to smoke during the treatment period. The McGuire and Vallance technique also used a "portable" shock apparatus that the patient could take home, to self-administer punishment under natural conditions. This technique may be a valuable step toward elimination of the artificiality of the usual treatment setting.

Wolpe (1964) used a technique that provided punishment for a response whenever it occurred in the patient's normal environment. A drug addict used self-punishment from a take-home shock device. The patient shocked himself whenever he noticed a craving for the drug. Although drug taking is accompanied by certain external stimulus referants, the instructions did not imply production of an image of these. There are no obvious external referants of "craving," although the response is presumably tied to a number of environmental cues. The technique can be described as punishment, in which part of the response punished is an early component of the behavior to be suppressed. The Wolpe portable device has the advantage that treatment can be administered by the patient in the situation in which the response to be suppressed actually occurs, and treatment is available as needed. Mees (1966) also used a patient-operated device in treatment of sadistic fantasies. The problem of relapsed patients, who are usually counted as failures in the studies reported here, may be more easily handled if continuing treatment is available as wanted outside the treatment setting.

Careful measurement of behavior change is uncommon in punishment studies with nonpsychotic patients. Many reports are presented as case studies, with no specific data provided. A few studies do provide more adequate information. Response rate was observed and recorded in

Wolpe's (1964) treatment of the drug addict who used a take-home shock device to punish himself for craving for the drug. Mees (1966) measured frequency of masturbation in a sadist for a period of nearly a year. Masturbation frequency with and without sadistic fantasies was obtained. A falloff rate of masturbation with sadistic fantasy was seen after a series of treatments during which the patient was shocked after producing sadistic fantasies on cue from the therapist. Influences on response rate from outside activities can be seen in the data for both these patients, making the rates less regular than might be found under well-controlled laboratory conditions.

In conclusion, these punishment procedures include several valuable techniques, and some that are perhaps not so desirable. A procedure using punishment might profitably borrow from the following list of features: the behavior punished should be a close approximation to the actual behavior to be suppressed in the outside environment; the procedure should be sufficiently simple so that the relevant behavioral process can be functionally described; the procedure should not include processes that facilitate the establishment of discriminations between the training setting and the outside environment; punishment should be given for the earliest detectable part of the behavior that is to be suppressed; and, if possible, it would be desirable to suppress the behavior in the presence of those environmental stimuli that control it in order to eliminate the behavioral control exercised by these stimuli. Finally, in many of the studies, collection of more adequate data on the process of behavior change would have been desirable, and can be recommended for future work.

Escape and Avoidance

Schizophrenic children. The first study to be described here illustrates the steps involved in escape-avoidance learning with schizophrenic children. The study was carried out on the two five-year-old identical twins who were described in the preceding section. Of particular importance is the fact that they were without social responsiveness, even though they had been treated in an inpatient setting for one year prior to this study. The procedure has been more fully described elsewhere (Lovaas, Schaeffer, & Simmons, 1965c). Data on this learning are presented in Figure 5. This figure gives the proportion of time the children responded to the adults' commands (proportion of Rs to SDs) of "come

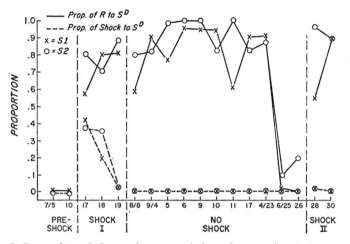

FIG. 5. Proportion of time twins responded to the experimenter's commands (proportion of R to S^D) in relation to shock administration, and proportion of shock to S^D (commands).

here." As can be seen, in the two pre-shock sessions, the children did not respond. During the first three shock sessions (shock 1) the children learned to respond to the adults' requests within the prescribed time interval and thus avoided shock. The procedure was as follows: there were two adults in the room with the child. The child stood barefooted on a grid floor which could be instantly electrified. In the escape phase of training, consisting of 50 trials, the two adults faced each other, about 3 feet apart, with the child standing (held, if necessary) between them so that he faced one of the adults. This adult would lean forward, stretch his arms out, and say "come here." At the same time shock was turned on and remained on until the child moved in the direction of this adult, or, if the child had not moved within 3 seconds, until the second adult pushed the child in the direction of the inviting adult. Either type of movement of the child immediately terminated the shock. The child had to walk alternately from one adult to the other. In the avoidance sessions that followed the adult would withhold the shock contingent upon the child's approach. At the same time the cues for approach were gradually faded until the adults, on opposite sides of the room, merely said "come here," without turning or otherwise signalling the child. It is important to translate this procedure in clinical terms: the contingencies are made very explicit to the child; if his repertoire is deficient in escaping the stress he is given help; this help is gradually removed.

The changed responsiveness of the children to the adults' requests was maintained for the subsequent nine months with no shock sessions. There was a relatively sudden decrease in both children's responsiveness after nine months, i.e., the social behavior of coming to the adult extinguished. One noncontingent shock, however, immediately reinstated the social responsiveness (shock 2), suggesting that the children responded to it as a discriminative stimulus for social behavior. The ease with which the children acquired this behavior, its durability, and the generalized behavior changes in the children (which will be described later) encouraged further use of aversive stimuli for motivational purposes.

The next three cases illustrate the use of escape-avoidance procedures, but with a more complicated response than that involved in physically approaching attending adults, namely language and intellectual behaviors. We discuss *Pamela* first. She had an extensive history of prior treatment, having been seen in psychoanalytically-oriented treatment for four years (from the time she was two and one-half years of age), followed by two years of residential treatment, but without change in her very psychotic status. When she came to us she engaged in self-stimulatory behaviors, including crossing of the eyes and grotesque movements of the mouth, with a protruding tongue, up to 99% of the day. In her favor, she had echolalic speech and liked to be cuddled and held by attending adults.

She progressed rather well, especially in the language area where an extensive program was devised for her. In particular, she had learned to suppress her echolalic speech and had acquired a correct usage of prepositions, color, shape, and many other abstract terms, and had begun some early intellectual work such as alphabet recognition and elementary arithmetic. Most of the children we have seen maintain the acquired behaviors when reinforcement is shifted from food to social stimulation sometime during the first year of treatment. Unlike these, Pamela regressed to her early psychotic behavior whenever food was removed as a reward, in spite of her apparent liking for attention. On a clinical level Pamela gave the impression that she was completely without any form of anxiety, and oblivious to her failures. It was decided then that should she become more anxious about her inadequacies, which might be accomplished by punishing her for her failures, she would be able to maintain more appropriate functioning without the use of food. It seems reasonable that most normal children would experience anxiety about behaving in a bizarre manner, and failing (or refusing) to answer correctly in the presence of adults. The administration of aversive stimulation could perhaps help Pamela achieve some of the feelings of normal children.

The study of Pamela is summarized in Figure 6. Two kinds of be-

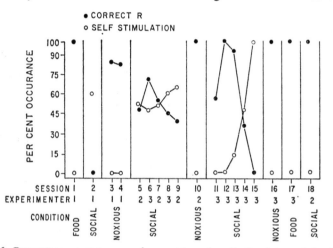

FIG. 6. Percentage occurrence of correct and self-stimulatory behavior in Pamela as a function of various operations given on the ordinate.

haviors were recorded: self-stimulation, which included flapping of the arms, rocking, grotesque facial expressions, including crossing of the eyes, and hoarse meaningless laughter. At the same time correct behavior on her part was also recorded. This included labeling of colors when requested to do so, and identifying objects by their appropriate names. Both the color and object-labeling were behaviors that had been mastered by Pamela for quite some time. Three experimenters were involved in this study; all had worked with Pamela extensively for more than 2 hours a day over the previous six months. It can be observed that in session 1, when food is used as a reinforcement, Pamela's correct behavior was virtually 100%, while her psychotic self-stimulatory behavior was zero. As soon as the experimenters shifted to social rewards her correct behavior fell to zero while her self-stimulatory rose to 60%. In sessions 3 and 4 Experimenter 1 gave Pamela noxious stimuli (slap on the thigh) contingent upon self-stimulatory behavior, and removed the noxious stimuli contingent upon correct behavior. It can be observed that the self-stimulation dropped immediately to zero and that the correct behavior rose to above 80%. This, then, is very similar to her behavior during food reinforcement, and points to the interchangeability of food and aversive stimuli as basic reinforcers. In the next five sessions (sessions 5 through 9) she was cared for by Experimenter 2 and 3, who used only social reinforcers. It appears here that there is some generalization from Experimenter 1 to Experimenters 2 and 3 but that she acquired a discrimination over time—she started to "fall apart." In session 10 Experimenter 2 replicated the operations of Experimenter 1 with the same results. In sessions 11 through 15 it is apparent that while initially there is some generalization from Experimenters 1 and 2 to Experimenter 3, this extinguishes over time. Experimenter 3, in session 16, replicated Experimenters 1 and 2 in applying aversive stimuli, and with the same results. Session 18 was a check on the preceding learning. In this session Experimenter 2 used merely social reinforcers (approval) and despite this the child was very appropriate. Her behavior in session 18 contrasted markedly to her behavior in sessions prior to aversive stimuli (session 2) where social reinforcement alone yielded no correct or appropriate behavior and a large amount of self-stimulatory behavior. An instance of aversive stimulation with Pamela is recorded in the film "Reinforcement Therapy[4]" and the changes discussed here can be observed more fully in that film.

The case of *Jimmy* demonstrates the same interchangeability of the effects of food and noxious stimuli on a previously learned response. Jimmy was an eleven-year-old autistic boy who, with the exception of being mute, had striking similarities to Pamela. He had received extensive, prior, psychoanalytically-oriented treatment with no noticeable improvement, and maintained the same lethargic, anxiety-free life. Figure 7 shows the results of a study with Jimmy using aversive stimuli. The particular task involved here was very similar to Pamela's, requiring Jimmy to correctly label pictures of objects, a previously mastered task. During sessions 1 through 5, which represent blocks of 30 trials and a spread over several days, it can be observed that as much as four requests (SDs) were needed in order for him to give his answer to a question he knew very well. During sessions 6 through 10 noxious stimuli in the form of slaps on the thigh were given if he failed to respond on first presentation of the question; he could avoid addi-

---

4. Smith, Kline, & French, 1966.

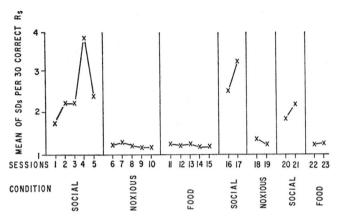

Fɪɢ. 7. Mean number of S^Ds (Experimenter's requests) needed for correct answers (Rs) in Jimmy.

tional aversive stimuli by giving his answer when asked. As can be observed, he did much better on this task when under the threat of punishment. In sessions 11 through 15 he received food reinforcement contingent upon correct behavior; no aversive stimulation was employed here, and it can be seen that his behavior during sessions using food and noxious stimulation was virtually identical. The adequacy of performance fell apart again when social approval was reintroduced during sessions 16 and 17. Subsequent sessions were replications of the preceding ones and speak for the reliability of the findings. It should be pointed out that Jimmy and Pamela are not typical of the schizophrenic children we have seen, where often it has been possible to shift from food to social rewards over time without any concurrent disruption in behavior.

The case of *Kevin* is the most dramatic example of effects of aversive stimuli we have seen. Kevin was six years old at the beginning of treatment. He had received prior psychoanalytically-oriented treatment for two years and was referred to UCLA by his therapist because he had failed to show adequate improvement. He was effectively mute, although he had occasionally been overheard to engage in appropriate speech involving as much as three-word phrases. This occurred on an average of once a week and never upon the request of others. He was generally oblivious to other people except when they demanded behaviors of him, at which point he became extremely negativistic. He had no appropriate play, but on the other hand he did not engage in the self-stimulatory behaviors typical of schizophrenic children. During the first four months he was reinforced with food for his attempts at correct imitation of the attending adult's speech. He had two behaviors that seemed directly in defiance of the attending adult's attempts to work with him; he would cover his ears with his hands when spoken to, and attempt to move out of his chair whenever the formal language training took place. He was therefore reinforced with food for taking his hands off his ears when requested to do so, and for sitting in the chair when an adult addressed him. Despite four months of imitation training Kevin made no progress whatsoever. This failure to improve on all accounts, even in the simple behavior of sitting still, was judged to be due to the effect of reinforcers other than food, since all children previously seen had acquired such simple behaviors. In other words, it appeared that Kevin was extremely reinforced by doing the opposite of what his teachers wanted him to do.

It was decided, therefore, to punish him for his negativistic behavior, and to withdraw these aversive stimuli contingent upon his complying with the adult's requests. Since we did not know whether he had in fact a major problem of some organic nature that prevented him from making progress in speech, it was decided to restrict use of aversive stimuli to training Kevin to sit on a chair and to take his hands off his ears. During the first five days on this regimen, he received a loud "no" and a slap on the thigh if he moved off the designated chair, or if he failed to take his hands off his ears when asked to do so. He was seen for 3 hours a day during this time, and despite rather extensive corporal punishment, to the point where Kevin's skin was bruised and the adult was completely exhausted, he only seemed to get worse; that is, he moved off the chair more often, and covered his ears with his hands almost all of the time. It was apparent that the adult's anger and corporal punishment served, paradoxically, as positive reinforcers for Kevin. At that point it was decided to use electric shock, which was administered through two electrodes pasted on his buttock. The contingencies were the same as before; shock was delivered contingent upon disobeying the adult's commands, but not if he failed to imitate appropriately. The results of shock were in startling contrast with corporal punishment. Kevin became very afraid: he would cry and shiver, and his defiance stopped within the first 10 minutes. He immediately initiated very good eye-to-face contact with the attending adult. By the end of the first day (2 hours) he imitated 100% correctly on the tasks where he had not improved during the prior four months. On the second day the imitation demands were doubled, without any problem. Fourteen days later he was correctly imitating 35 sounds (mostly English words, some having a two-syllable structure). Shock was discontinued at that point, and his speech has been increasing ever since. In view of the extensive base-line extending over more than four months, the results of the previous psychotherapy, and the very sudden change contingent upon electric shock, it is appropriate to attribute the change in Kevin's behavior to the shock.

All these studies, and those to be reviewed later in this section, used aversive stimuli in a contingent manner. We can present some data from recently initiated studies on the use and effect of noncontingent aversive stimulation. An illustrative case (a more complete description of this case is presented by Perloff & Lovaas, 1967) [5] is that of *Billy*, who was a five-year-old schizophrenic mute child when the imitation training program was begun with him. At the beginning of this training he would imitate rather well but only when he received food or escaped aversive stimuli as reinforcers. Clinically, like Pamela and Jimmy, he appeared to be devoid of anxiety. One study of noncontingent aversive stimulation lasted 98 days, with a 20-minute session being run each day. During this time the proportion of correct and incorrect behavior was recorded on each of ten verbal imitative tasks over the various experimental treatments. Figure 8 shows that, during the first four sessions when he received food as reinforcement, his correct behavior was high and his incorrect behavior was low. The next sessions (6 through 22), when food was withdrawn as a reinforcer, show a gradual decrease in the proportion of correct behavior. Social reinforcement failed to alter this low rate, as can be seen in sessions 24 through 26. In session 28 he was given noncontingent aversive stimuli (slap on the buttocks) which immediately reinstated a high level of correct behavior. Sessions 30 to 34, when the aversive stimuli were removed, show an extinction of its effectiveness. Session 36 replicated session 28. Sessions 38 through 56 represent the second extinction of those effects. When the aversive stimuli were presented for the third time, during sessions 58 through 64, they did not produce the previous effects. Instead, the amount of correct behavior went down while incorrect behavior rose. The rise in incorrect behavior at this time is in

5. Perloff, B., & Lovaas, O.I. Effect of non-contingent aversive stimulation on learned behaviors in an autistic child. Unpublished manuscript, 1967.

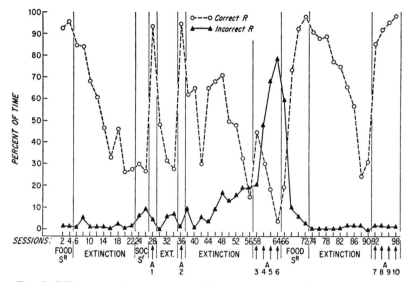

Fᴵɢ. 8. Billy's percentage correct and incorrect imitative behavior as a function of various operations: food S^R (reinforcement), social S^r (reinforcement), A (non-contingent aversive stimulation).

contrast to previous sessions when correct and incorrect behavior both stay down. It seemed reasonable to suppose he had lost (forgotten) his previous discriminations (it was more than 60 days since he had last been trained on these). Therefore, correct responding was reinstated, using food as a reinforcer (sessions 66 through 72). The effect of food reinforcement was extinguished in sessions 74 through 90 and this time, when the noncontingent aversive stimulation was reintroduced (sessions 92 through 98), correct responding reappeared. This supports the notion that Billy's failure to improve and his actual increase in incorrect behavior, with the use of aversive stimuli (sessions 58 through 64), was based on loss of the appropriate discriminations.

The main point of Figure 8 is that noncontingent aversive stimulation, or anxiety, which it probably would be called in a more clinical sense, is likely to be helpful to a patient insofar as he knows what he is supposed to do. Otherwise, the aversive stimulation is discriminative for an increase in behavior in general, including incorrect behavior. These data would not have been obtained if the aversive stimulation had been used in contingent form, for example, in an escape-avoidance paradigm. Finally, the interchangeability of food and aversive stimulation in Billy's case replicated the data from Jimmy and Pamela.

Nonpsychotic patients. We turn now to some other uses of aversive stimulation using an avoidance paradigm. In a series of articles, Feldman, MacCulloch, and colleagues (Feldman & MacCulloch, 1964; MacCulloch, Feldman, & Pinschof, 1965; MacCulloch, Feldman, Orford & MacCulloch; Feldman, MacCulloch, Mellor, & Pinschof, 1966) have developed and investigated a form of avoidance training for treatment of homosexuality. They also used a relief stimulus to train "approach" responses to heterosexual stimuli.

The problem of extinction was noted by Feldman and MacCulloch (1964) as the principal reason for the use of an avoidance technique. Feldman and MacCulloch examined the learning literature for extinction effects under various avoidance training procedures. On the basis of results such as those described in Solomon and Brush (1956) on traumatic avoidance, they selected anticipatory avoidance training as showing the greatest resistance to extinction. Among the techniques examined were: classical (respondent) conditioning (in which avoidance is measured in motor responding on occasional trials when the aversive UCS is not presented); simple punishment; and prior anxiety conditioning, in which classical trials using an aversive UCS are followed by training in which an avoidance response is made available. Feldman and MacCulloch concluded that these methods yield easy extinction in comparison with the resistance to extinction shown after anticipatory avoidance training.

The Feldman and MacCulloch procedure was fully described, and a considerable amount of data on the results of the treatment is available. We will examine the procedure used and some of the results in considerable detail, to determine some of the effective variables that may be present in the application of avoidance procedures.

Briefly, the procedure involved use of slides of attractive nude males, shown to the homosexual patients. After a few seconds the slides were removed and shock was given. The patients could avoid shock by pressing a button to remove the slide before shock onset. Other details of the procedure will be given shortly.

Feldman and MacCulloch argued that classical conditioning showed rapid extinction when the aversive stimulus was removed. This appears to imply that classical conditioning would be a generally unsatisfactory therapeutic technique, although as the next section will show, this paradigm has been used extensively with aversive stimulation. However, the Feldman and MacCulloch argument for the superiority of avoidance conditioning, and specifically anticipatory avoidance training, raises several questions.

First, they appear to have ignored considerable data on extinction from studies that used variations of the techniques they reject. Prior anxiety conditioning, for example, has been recently advocated by Turner and Solomon (1962) as an optimal avoidance procedure for producing strong resistance to extinction. Turner and Solomon regard strong emotional conditioning as an essential element in avoidance learning, and in preserving the acquired response from extinction. Thus, in prior anxiety conditioning procedure, the use of preliminary classical (non-avoidance) trials should give the emotional response opportunity to become strongly conditioned to the warning stimuli, before avoidance learning is begun. Simple punishment for operant responses, also rejected by Feldman and MacCulloch, is known now to produce complete and permanent suppression of responding in some situations (Azrin & Holz, 1966), although references concerning early work have often given the impression that punishment could not create lasting effects. The Feldman and MacCulloch conclusions, derived from specific studies, cannot be generalized to cover the techniques in all variations.

A second problem in the Feldman and MacCulloch argument is that they based their conclusion on a comparison of ease of extinction among techniques that typically use different extinction procedures, and not only different acquisition procedures. After simple punishment, for example, extinction involves re-acquisition of the prepunished base rate. Re-acquisition takes place under conditions of positively reinforced responding. Similarly, for classical conditioning, extinction of learned operants involves the disappearance of skeletal responses attached to the CS, during repeated CS presentations without reinforcement. (The comments by Feldman and MacCulloch on extinction appear to refer to extinction of operant components only.) These skeletal responses typically do not greatly curtail or modify the CS, in extinction after classical training, as they do in most avoidance procedures. Finally, anticipatory avoidance training or prior anxiety conditioning involves disappearance of a learned avoidance response to the warning CS. The response is one that eliminated or modified this stimulus during training, and continues to do so during extinction. Thus these different behaviors during extinction trials produce quite different consequences. An external CS may or may not occur, and a well-learned escape response to the CS, if the CS does occur, may or may not be available.

If various acquisition techniques are to be meaningfully compared for resistance to extinction, analysis of the situations in which extinction trials occur is needed (Marx, 1966). It is clear that for both alcoholics and homosexuals the environmental circumstances in which exposure to the aversive stimuli occur are not simply like those in laboratory extinction trials, for which the stimulus is presented but the aversive stimulation is removed. Numerous avoidance or escape responses to aversive stimuli will be available in the outside environment that were unavailable in the training setting, and these responses may occur with high probability to an aversive stimulus to which they have not been specifically trained (Solomon & Turner, 1962).

As a consequence of these difficulties, it seems unclear how the Feldman and MacCulloch procedure for avoidance training will bring about superior resistance to extinction in the outside environment. Nor is it clear what learned response it is that is to be trained to resist extinction effects. Numerous behaviors of avoidance and escape from aversive stimuli are presumably part of everyone's repertoire. The avoidance response provided in the Feldman and MacCulloch procedure, a button press and a spoken word, is unlike responses that are likely to be successful in avoiding or escaping post-treatment stimuli. The preservation of this response from extinction would serve little purpose.

In reply to these criticisms, it might be supposed that what is being accomplished in this procedure is learning of avoidance of particular stimuli, and that response generalization will provide a mechanism for transference to avoidance responses appropriate to various particular occasions. Feldman and MacCulloch do not present data from the learning literature to support an expectation for such response generalization. A second possible supposition is that anticipatory avoidance training would produce resistance to extinction superior to, for example, classical training, even if extinction trials were carried out in the same manner in both cases—in circumstances that are different from those present in training, and for which the learned avoidance response does not effectively avoid. The usual procedures for observing extinction in avoidance studies are not satisfactory sources of data to support this proposition. These difficulties imply that emphasis on the operant response acquired in training, rather than on the aversive character of the conditioned stimuli, is not justified when the training and post-training conditions have the disparities noted here.

Feldman and MacCulloch included a number of features that depart from typical avoidance training procedures. Before commenting on these, the training will be described in more detail. Patients (homosexual males) were seated in a darkened room in front of a screen on which slides were projected from the rear. Slides were shown of males, nude or semi-nude, that the patient had prejudged to be of varying degrees of attractiveness. The patient was told to leave each slide on as long as he found it attractive. He was told that he could remove the slide by pressing a switch and saying "no." If he did not avoid in 8 seconds (timing varied around this figure), he received an electric shock until he did so. Shock was presented at a level the patient had previously selected as extremely unpleasant, and was varied somewhat during training. After three consecutive successful avoidances a new schedule was introduced. For this schedule, one-third of the trials were as described before. For another one-third of the trials the patient always received a shock, and could not remove the CS even though he made the designated avoidance response. On the remaining third, the avoidance response succeeded, but the removal of the CS was delayed for a brief period. The three kinds of trials were alternated randomly. On all trials, including delayed trials, the response required for avoidance was a single switch press, although others may well have occurred.

The use of unavoidable shock on one-third of the trials was designed to increase resistance to extinction by providing partial reinforcement, but this procedure constitutes an unusual partial reinforcement condition. Avoidance training in itself provides partial reinforcement since not all CS occurrences are punished if avoidance responses are occasionally made. But here, on some trials, the patient fails to avoid aversive stimulation, even with the proper avoidance response, since shock is delivered on one-third of the trials even for a consistently avoiding subject. The presence of these unavoidable shock trials provides the mechanism for aversion conditioning, and thus raises the possibility that classically conditioned aversion is the effective agent in the success of the procedure.

The acquisition of an aversion, or emotional response, to the stimulus does not appear to have been considered important by these authors. The shock intensity used does not seem to be as great as that described by

Turner and Solomon (1962). Shock intensity is an important parameter in the acquisition of an emotional response, as measured by a suppression ratio (Kamin & Schaub, 1963). The Feldman and MacCulloch procedure is thus not traumatic avoidance.

An unusual feature in the Feldman and MacCulloch technique concerns the instructions to the patient. Instructions made the nature of the avoidance response (a button press) clear, and the CS-UCS interval was long enough to make perfect responding quite feasible. Patients were given the additional instruction to continue to look at the CS as long as it was attractive. This instruction has no analogue in avoidance training with lower animals.

MacCulloch, *et al.*, (1965) presented a sample of the extensive data taken during the course of avoidance-relief training. The authors wished to see if the avoidance latency would duplicate results obtained by Solomon and Wynne (1953) and Turner and Solomon for traumatic learning in dogs and humans. Response latencies for the avoidance response and pulse rate changes to the conditioned aversive stimulus (projected pictures) were collected over trials.

Data from four exemplary cases were examined for features that might be predictive of later outcomes. Two of these patients maintained a revised sexual orientation, as of a one-year follow-up; one patient apparently relapsed after three months; and one was unchanged by treatment. Avoidance latencies for the two most successful cases decreased rapidly during the first session. For these subjects, latencies long enough to produce shock were rare: only one occurred for one subject, the other received about five over all sessions. The relapsed patient received more shocks for slow responding than these first two cases, but he received none after the first three sessions. The unsuccessfully treated patient began session 1 with very fast responses, and avoided throughout sessions 3 through 7, but did not avoid at all in sessions 2 or 8 (the last). For all subjects, as noted previously, shocks were given on the one-third of the trials for which the avoidance responses were not effective in removing the slide.

Sample pulse rate changes to the CS were presented for two of these four patients: one of the two successful cases, and the patient for whom treatment failed. The data, on inspection, showed pulse rate changes to the CS occurred only in the former patient. This variable may provide a usable measure of the effectiveness of the classical conditioning contingencies present on the one-third of the trials with unavoidable shock. The apparent absence of pulse rate changes in the subject considered a failure may be due to the failure of the slides to become strong conditioned aversive stimuli, rather than, as one of the suggestions offered by the authors, to a lack of responsiveness of this patient on this response measure. The patient was described as poorly motivated and deceptive, and may have overstated his reaction to the shock intensity (not given) that he had selected as being "highly unpleasant," and thus had received as the UCS on training trials. Feldman and MacCulloch were apparently not concerned with the emotional or aversive conditioning that might be occurring in their treatment, and did not investigate these possibilities.

The relationship between autonomic responses and avoidance responses is unclear (McAllister & McAllister, 1965). Turner and Solomon speculated that an emotional (or visceral or respondent or fear) reaction may be a necessary precondition for the occurrence of avoidance responding. Whether strong conditioned aversion is a necessity for avoidance in humans may be questioned. Human subjects can certainly perform avoidance responses on instruction or other cues without actual experience of the experimental UCS. Subjects may also produce autonomic responses to a stimulus if they observe or are informed that the stimulus will be followed by an aversive stimulus such as shock (Berger, 1962), that is, without actually experiencing the contingencies of the situation. Whatever the mechanisms by which responses may be acquired in this latter situation, they may likely not show the strength of responses acquired through actual exposure to the unconditioned aversive stimulus.

The fourth patient, who showed no improvement, but who avoided successfully in six of eight sessions and who did not avoid at all in the two others, gave an indication that the latency measure used here may have been contaminated by some extra-treatment factors. Instructions were given to leave the slide on as long as it was attractive. Such instructions may indicate to the patient that the time the slide is left on serves as a cue for the therapist, in the same way that verbal comments do, since it provides the therapist with a report of the patient's experience. The unsuccessful patient who did not avoid throughout two sessions may have been using long latencies in these sessions as a cue to the therapist that he was not experiencing change as a result of the therapy. In any case, such possibilities cannot be ignored in experimentation involving social communication processes. Other voluntary measures may have similar problems.

MacCulloch, *et al.*, (1966) extended the avoidance-relief technique to alcoholism, and reported data for four unsuccessful cases. Pulse rate data, available from only two cases, showed no obvious evidence of conditioning. Latency data were judged more variable than that obtained for successfully treated homosexual patients.

A further measure, taken in connection with the work on homosexuals, was reported by Feldman *et al.* (1966). A scale was used to measure change in homosexuals in sexual attitudes toward men and women. The two statements "men (women) are sexually to me . . ." were completed, for a large series of paired endings, by selecting one member from each pair. Each pair consisted of two degrees of a single descriptive term; for example, "quite beautiful" paired with "very beautiful." The questionnaire was administered at the beginning and middle of therapy, and at intervals after, for 32 patients in the therapy previously described. Measures of homosexual and heterosexual interest were derived from the results. The group was divided into 23 "improved" and 9 "unimproved" on the basis of other evidence, and their scores were compared. The unimproved group showed little change in ratings, whereas the improved group showed change in the expected direction in both statements. Other checks on consistency and reliability were made with favorable results.

Avoidance training has been used in one other study treating homosexuality (Clark, 1965), using a rather simpler technique. As in the Feldman and MacCulloch work, the avoidance response used has little relevance to responses that might bring about successful avoidance or escape in situations outside the laboratory or in the patient's everyday life.

Some procedures have been able to use avoidance responses that are appropriate for the situations in which the behavior problem occurs. Examples are the work of Liversedge and Sylvester (1955), and Sylvester and Liversedge (1960) on occupational cramps, and in Lovibond (1963, 1964), and others, on enuresis.

Lovibond used the "twin-signal" apparatus, a variation of the Mowrer and Mowrer (1938) apparatus for waking the child at the first evidence of wetting. The device sounds a 1-second warning when the specially-constructed pad on which the child sleeps becomes damp. If the signal is not heeded, a more aversive stimulus follows. If successful, the technique results in retention of urine while in bed. The resulting behavior change appears to be due to discriminated avoidance. Usual urination during the day provides discrimination training for conditions free of aversive consequences. An advantage of this treatment of enuresis is that it takes place in the patient's bed, in the presence of the appropriate home-environment cues, rather than in the laboratory.

Liversedge and Sylvester treated writer's cramp (tremors and spasm) by requiring subjects to write with, and otherwise to manipulate, a pen-like instrument in a steady and programmed manner. The apparatus used was such that variations from the task due to tremors or spasms were automatically punished with electric shock. As in the work on enuresis the appropriate avoidance response during treatment is quite similar to the appropriate post-treatment response. Thus the operant training may be expected to transfer readily from the training setting.

ESTABLISHMENT OF STIMULUS FUNCTIONS

We have earlier noted the value of establishing or altering stimulus functions. Let us briefly elaborate on those comments at this point. If one views psychopathological behavior in learning theory terms, the emphasis can be placed either on deviations in behavioral development or in the acquisition of functions. For example, an abnormality might be defined as a failure to achieve speech behavior, or the learning of inappropriate drinking behavior. On the other hand, a deviation may be viewed as a distortion in acquisition of normal stimulus functions; for example, a person for whom interpersonal closeness had no function might be defined as deviant. Since acquisitions of behaviors and functions are defined in terms of one another, it would be difficult to alter stimulus functions without simultaneously altering behaviors, and vice versa. However, the operations which govern the acquisition of behaviors are different from those that regulate stimulus functions. The use of one of these operations as a therapeutic intervention would require a treatment program of different construction than would the use of the other.

Most of the work with nonpsychotic patients reviewed in this section has concentrated on establishing aversions to specific stimuli. The intended function of the acquired aversion is to eliminate undesirable behavioral repertoires controlled by these stimuli. As an example, an alcoholic may be exposed to the taste and odor of alcohol, as a CS, followed by an intense aversive stimulus, in a classical conditioning procedure. The indirect behavior change intended is elimination of alcoholism, but concommitant behavior changes are desirable and occur if treatment is successful, since probably much other behavior is tied in with the specific drinking activity.

The need for the acquisition of other, more normal, stimulus functions in this case is perhaps less obvious than it is for schizophrenic children, who often lack appropriate behaviors almost entirely. In these children, aversive stimulation is valuable for building positive reinforcers, as well as negative ones, in the attempt to overcome their behavioral deficiencies.

A stimulus discriminative for, or associated with, the termination of a primary aversive stimulus may acquire the properties of a positive reinforcer. The conditions under which such reinforcing properties will be acquired by stimuli associated with shock offset have received considerable critical and experimental attention (Beck, 1961; Verhave, 1962; Dinsmoor & Clayton, 1966). There are many failures to produce the effect. As an example, Mowrer and Aiken (1954) measured the responses to a CS, after training in which the CS onset had been timed to coincide with shock termination. The index used was change in response rate when the CS was introduced during bar-pressing for food. If the CS had acquired positive reinforcing properties, it was reasoned, then it should facilitate bar-pressing; but suppression rather than facilitation occurred, indicating that the CS evoked a fear reaction. The authors suggested that if testing were done with fear present the expected secondary reinforcing effect might be seen.

The foregoing would imply that these conditioned reinforcing stimuli are most strongly reinforcing in stressful conditions. If these stimuli were to be other people in the patient's environment, then these people would function as "relief" stimuli, to reduce fearfulness associated with aversive events. However, even if this were so, training to approach people during stressful situations may allow the people to become salient cues for delivery of other positive reinforcers, and thus to extend their social and affective value for the patient in whom the approach responses were established.

Stimulus functions in schizophrenic children. We consider, in line with Ferster's hypothesis (1961), that the deficiencies in the acquisition of social behaviors, in children, can be accounted for by postulating a deficiency in the acquisition of social stimulus functions. This implies need for investigation of the conditions under which the environment of schizophrenic children can acquire stimulus functions for them.

Although schizophrenic children are deficient in a large number of stimulus functions, such as those which elicit emotional behavior, the primary concern in the data to be presented here has been with those functions that can be conditioned in such a manner as to facilitate acquisition or extinction of operant behaviors.

The first study in this area has been reported more fully elsewhere (Lovaas, *et al.*, 1965c). The study dealt with the establishment of "no" as a negative reinforcer. The twins who provided the data in Figures 4 and 5 were taught a lever-pressing response for candy and were tested for the suppressing power of the word "no" on rate of responding. The data are given in Figure 9. As can be observed, when "no" is presented

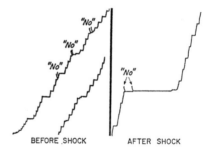

BEFORE SHOCK   AFTER SHOCK

FIG. 9. Lever-pressing for candy as cumulative response curves: effect of "no" on lever-pressings by one twin before and after "no" was paired with shock onset.

contingent upon bar-pressing prior to its pairing with shock, it has no effect upon the child's behavior (the record of only one child is presented here; the other record is the same). After the word "no" had been paired with shock, it acquired suppressing properties. It is noteworthy that this was the first time that these children had been observed to respond to the word "no."

This finding, the conditioning of aversive stimuli, has since been replicated over a large number of children. In general, the effect of such stimuli seem almost identical to those of the unconditioned, or primary, ones. This observation is illustrated very well in the case of Linda, the same patient who provided the data in Figure 3. While attempting to suppress Linda's self-destructive behavior in one situation (in a room), the word "no" was paired with electric shock. Subsequently, the word was used to suppress her self-destructive behavior in another situation (during a walk). The data on that suppression are presented in Figure 10. As can be observed, there were no systematic changes in self-destruc-

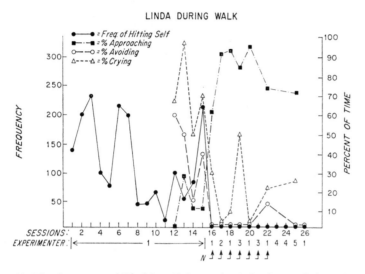

FIG. 10. The frequency of Linda's self-destructive behavior, and the percentage of approaching and avoiding the attending adult, and crying, during walks as a function of the presentation of N (the word "no") and the particular experimenter involved.

tive behavior during the first 15 days of base-line data. On the 16th day the word "no" ("N" on the abscissa) was given contingent upon such behavior with immediate suppressing effects. The similarity in the effects of the conditioned and the unconditioned suppressor is readily apparent by comparison of figures 10 and 3, in terms of both the response suppression and the generalized behavior change.

We have previously discussed the rationale for use of aversive stimuli to build positive reinforcers, and it is sufficient here to state that one might consider such events, the association of social stimuli with the termination of pain, as essential for the acquisition of social bonds. It is quite plausible that children become fond of their parents, not because the parents are presenters of primary reinforcers, but because they mediate the termination of pain. This argument is strengthened when one considers the pervasiveness of pain and anxiety in human existence. It is present from infancy. The good parent acts to rescue his child from discomfort—a parent is safety. Such rescues allow for the acquisition of positive reinforcers. The pervasiveness of discomfort virtually guarantees maintenance (non-extinction) of reinforcing functions based on pain reduction. It follows that a child who did not experience this basic pain and anxiety would also be deficient in social reinforcers, as well as the social behaviors that normally obtain such reinforcing consequences. Many psychotic children seem devoid of anxiety—the less anxiety the more severe the "regression." Mowrer (1950) has discussed, in a somewhat similar vein, the possibility that such deficiencies may contribute to abnormal behavior in general.

To test for the possibility of establishing positive secondary reinforcers on the basis of their associations with withdrawal of primary negative reinforcement, the reinforcing properties of an adult were observed under the following conditions. Ten pretraining sessions were given, in which the child was reinforced for bar-pressing for candy and a 5-second exposure to the attending adult (a screen between the child and the attending adult was momentarily removed, placing the adult's face within the child's view). When the candy was removed as a reward for bar-pressing, even though the visual exposure to the adult was retained, the bar-pressing response extinguished; that is, the rate gradually decreased—the sight of the adult was an insufficient reinforcer for the child.

These pretraining sessions were followed by a set of experimental sessions, carried out in a different environment, where the attending adult rescued the child from pain; that is, shock would come on but would be terminated once the child turned to the adult, who would then comfort him. Immediately following this procedure the child was placed again in the bar-pressing situation, and a change in his rate of responding on the bar provided a test for any change in the reinforcing properties of the adult, subsequent to his being paired with shock reduction.

The data from this experiment are presented in Figure 11. The child's lever-pressing behavior is presented as cumulative curves. The last extinction curve from pretraining is labeled 1. This curve gives the rate of lever-pressing in the last extinction session preceding the adult's association with shock reduction. The upward-moving hatchmarks on the curves show the occasions on which the adult was visually presented to the child. The heavy vertical lines labeled shock show shock-escape

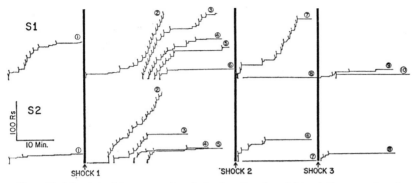

FIG. 11. The twins' lever-pressing behavior for the sight of the experimenter as a function of the experimenter's association with shock reduction (the curve labelled "1" is the last extinction curve from pretraining). Shock preceded sessions 2, 7 and 9 for S1, and sessions 2, 6, and 8 for S2. The upward-moving hatchmarks on the curves indicate occasions on which the experimenter was visually presented to *S*s.

training preceding sessions 2, 7, and 9 (for the first child, S1) and sessions 2, 6, and 8 for the second child (S2).

There was a substantial increase in the rate of lever-pressing for the sight of the adult accompanying shock-escape training for both children. The curves also show the extinction of this response, as would be expected. The extinction is apparent in the falling rate within shock sessions, as well as in the falling rate over the various shock sessions. The children's behavior in this regard was systematic and orderly. A more complete description of this experiment is given in another paper (Lovaas, *et al.,* 1965c).

Aversive conditioning in nonpsychotic patients. Extensive work has been done with classical conditioning procedures to establish aversion to specific stimuli related to alcoholism, for example, and also for some other problems noted in previous sections. The procedures are often considerably simpler than those used in punishment and escape/avoidance training. In general they are not concerned with shaping of more appropriate operants as part of treatment. Tests of the effects of the training, in achieved aversiveness of stimuli, are usually lacking.

The work of Voegtlin and others at Shadell Sanitarium in Seattle, Washington, begun in the 1930's, is among the earliest therapeutic uses of aversive stimulation within a learning context. By 1950 these authors could report on treatment of over 4,000 cases (Voegtlin & Lemere, 1940; Voegtlin & Broz, 1949; Lemere & Voegtlin, 1950). The patients were confirmed alcoholics who entered treatment voluntarily. The patients were exposed to the sight, smell, and taste of various alcoholic drinks after being given an emetic mixture including emetine, which produced a nauseous reaction. The patient was given a small sip of alcohol at the onset of the reaction, and further small amounts through the period of nausea. The odor and sight of the liquor were constantly present also.

After taking the emetic mixture the patient would typically experience nausea whether or not he cooperated freely in exposing himself to the conditioned stimuli associated with alcohol. The procedure is similar to that of Blake (1965), which was discussed under the section on punishment. Both include conditions for classical conditioning of aversiveness to alcohol; they differ in that the behavior engaged in by the subjects in Blake's study resembles somewhat more the behavior involved in drinking alcohol, while the behavior of Voegtlin's subjects is more a passive acceptance of the offered taste and odor of alcohol. The difference may well be insubstantial. Voegtlin's procedure does contain features involving punishment. That is, the patient's cooperation in placing himself in a situation in which aversive stimulation is delivered has the character of a punished response, as do the specific cooperative actions he takes preceding the aversive stimulation, such as sipping or sniffing alcohol. However, the aim of the procedure was the establishment of aversion to the stimuli immediately associated with drinking alcohol.

A soft drink was provided in the treatment room between sessions to provide discrimination training for other liquids. Voegtlin excluded extraneous stimulation from the treatment room as much as possible, by using subdued lighting and other controls, and requesting the patient to attend specifically to the alcoholic stimuli while nauseous.

Voegtlin's work showed care in experimentation and close attention to the learning principles of the time. An especially valuable feature was the extensive follow-up, made over a period of ten years and longer, and covering a large number of those treated; 4090 of 4468 cases (Lemere & Voegtlin, 1950). Unfortunately, no data were provided on the growth of aversion to the stimuli during training. Patients were given a variable number of treatments (2–10). The basis for the decision as to the number of treatments in individual cases was not given, but the development of aversion was observable in the emotional and escape reactions of the patient to the experimental stimuli and toward other similar stimuli.

Voegtlin repeated treatment for patients who experienced a single relapse, with results about as good as for the initial treatment (Lemere & Voegtlin, 1950). Outcome data for this work will be discussed in a later section.

Voegtlin's procedure has been repeated, with variations, in other studies of alcoholism. Franks (1958) has reviewed some of these. The Voegtlin procedure did not provide training in any explicit technique for coping with the emotional reaction aroused, and virtually neglected the problem of extinction or the maintenance of the acquired response in the post-treatment setting. It was with this problem that Feldman and Mac-Culloch (1964) were so concerned. The extinction problem is relevant for all aversion therapies which must achieve lasting results during a brief period. Some of its aspects will be discussed here.

First, it should be noted that Voegtlin's procedure did not include discrimination trials to differentiate the immediate taste and odor of alcohol from other stimuli associated with alcohol or alcoholic experiences. Stimuli such as bottles of liquor in grocery stores or photographs of liquor in advertisements may have become aversive during treatment. Aversion may also have developed for numerous situations intimately and idiosyncratically associated with the patient's past experiences. Voegtlin and Lemere (1940) report aversive reactions to alcoholic stimuli other than those in the training trials, as well as unanticipated stimulus generalizations, such as aversion to snuff. Thus, by generalization, the procedure may attach an aversive reaction not only to the taste and odor of alcohol, but also to numerous stimuli to which the patient will frequently be exposed in the post-treatment environment.

Aversion acquired to commonplace environmental stimuli will be vulnerable to modification through experience. Post-treatment exposures to stimuli that have become aversive in training need not be simply extinction or discrimination trials; the natural environment offers opportunities for escape and avoidance. Many such behaviors are presumably well learned and may become appropriately and quickly attached to a newly aversive stimulus, whether specifically trained or not. These reactions tend to preserve the aversiveness of the conditioned stimuli from the extinction effects of unavoidable exposure. However, exposures to some stimuli are probable under circumstances for which avoidance or escape responses are not available. These selective exposures and responses should result in gradual reshaping of behavior, with selective loss of the effectiveness of particular stimuli to evoke an aversive reaction, while others retain their aversive characteristics. This reshaping process should be least rapid for stimuli most readily avoided in the environment, or least frequently encountered, such as the actual taste and odor of alcohol, which may not be experienced even in situations in which numerous related stimuli are present.

The reshaping occurring after treatment will be complicated by the presence of reinforcers associated with alcoholism in the patient's past experience. The stimuli made aversive may be discriminative cues for such reinforcements in some instances, and exposure to the aversive stimuli may be the only readily available path to these reinforcers. Also, aversive stimuli may be produced as a by-product of behavior sequences that also produce or maintain a positively reinforcing state of affairs. For example, social reinforcers for the patient may occur almost exclusively in situations in which alcohol is present. These factors will influence the process of reshaping by which the specifically conditioned stimuli lose aversiveness. The reshaping process described above may be of great complexity, as these brief comments indicate, and cannot be reduced to a simple laboratory analogue.

The reshaping process described above may operate very rapidly, as can be seen from a report by Miller, Dvorak, and Turner (1960). Some patients who had acquired an apparent strong emotional reaction to alcohol relapsed by drinking very shortly after treatment, even though they reported afterward that they could barely hold the first drink down because of the nausea it produced. A similar observation was made by Morgenstern, *et al.* (1965) concerning transvestites, although the initial relapses in these cases were not always followed by further cross-dressing. In some cases patients report that relapse is due to hostility toward the therapist or anger resulting from the therapeutic manipulations encountered in treatment.

In the case of alcoholics, social influence from peers appears to be a common accompaniment of relapse. Social reinforcers may maintain pathological behaviors if the social environment is compatible with their occurrence. Some examples are the social peer-status that smoking may provide a young person, or the reinforcing value for the homosexual of membership in the homosexual community. The effectiveness of simple aversion training should be relatively poor for those behaviors that have become tied most integrally and pervasively to the person's social functioning.

In summary, many of the effective stimulus functions that have controlled alcoholic behavior are left unchanged by techniques that establish aversion to specific stimuli in a laboratory setting. These functions will severely test the effectiveness of the acquired aversion to maintain sobriety and to endure, while the alcoholic effects a reorganization of his behavior into a nonalcoholic life-pattern.

Modifications of Voegtlin's treatment, retaining the use of an emetic drug, have been used for treatment of fetishism and transvestism (Raymond & O'Keeffe, 1965; Raymond, 1956; Lavin, Thorpe, Barker, Blakemore, & Conway, 1961), homosexuality (James, 1962; Freund, 1960), and a variety of the above, as well as alcoholics (Oswald, 1962). All of these studies used an apomorphine mixture to induce nausea, and (usually) presented specific objects to which an aversive reaction was to become conditioned during the period of nausea. (Apomorphine had been tried and abandoned by Voegtlin, because of its narcotic effect. There are no data indicating the importance of this fact for these therapeutic procedures.)

The studies of Raymond (1956); Lavin, *et al.* (1961); James (1962); Oswald (1962); and Glynn and Harper (1961) used continuous treatments, day and night, at 2-hour intervals. This procedure must place an extraordinary strain on the patient. Reasons for this aspect of the technique are not made clear in any of the studies, and it does not seem justifiable from learning data. The method does have the advantage that outside discrimination trials cannot occur before the aversive reaction has been fully developed. However, much of the aversiveness of the procedure is not relevant to the objective of treatment. The generalized aversiveness of a non-stop procedure may act to deter many patients from entering treatment, from continuing, or from returning for retreatment after a relapse.

Some studies have used symbolic or imaginal stimuli rather than actual objects. In some studies stimuli were presented before or at the beginning of nausea and were withdrawn before the reaction subsided; in others they were simply present as a part of the treatment setting. Voegtlin's work appears to have been more careful than many of these studies in excluding irrelevant aspects of the setting from the stimuli to be associated with aversive stimulation.

In these studies using apomorphine, control of temporal contingencies is generally not precise. Even so, some aspects of the appropriate CS in these settings must have occasionally been salient at UCS onset. Conditioning to the relevant stimuli may occur even without careful temporal control, since precise timing of CS onset, and removal of the CS before UCS termination, are not necessary conditions for aversion conditioning to occur. Long CS-UCS intervals may yield effective conditioning (Kamin, 1965) and conditioning to static features of the stimulus setting is also observed (McAllister & McAllister, 1965).

The relative advantages of an emetic reaction and electric shock as aversive events have not been studied. Use of electric shock does make possible better experimental control. A number of possible advantages of shock have been discussed by Rachman (1964). Electric shock has been used in several studies involving an aversion conditioning technique. Those to be discussed are: Thorpe and Schmidt (1963); Thorpe, Schmidt, and Castell (1963); Thorpe, Schmidt, Brown, and Castell (1964); Marks, Rachman, and Gelder (1965); Kushner and Sandler (1966); Solyom and Miller (1965); and McGuire and Vallance (1964). An advantage of the more precise control obtainable from use of shock has been that the studies include several attempts to obtain measures of the response processes occurring during treatment.

Some difficulties in obtaining measures of response acquisition in these therapeutic techniques have already been discussed. In spite of such difficulties, measures are desirable to demonstrate which experimental parameters are operating effectively, and to provide observations on the specific individual's response to treatment. Perhaps the most common measures are those involving characteristics of an operant response. Two other classes of measures are autonomic records and ratings, by the patient or others, of subjective experiences or of behavior outside the training situation. These are the three classes of measures that were obtained in the Feldman and MacCulloch work previously discussed.

Latency of response measures are presented, although not systematically, by Marks, *et al.* (1965) and by Thorpe, *et al.*, (1963). In these studies patients were shocked when they signaled that they had clearly visualized a given scene or fantasy. Latencies from beginning of trial to signal appeared to increase over trials. Of course, both the fantasy-activity and the signal for shock are punished here.

Solyom and Miller (1965) took physiological measures of finger blood volume in homosexual patients who were shocked while viewing slides of nude male figures. The slides were present for about 60 seconds and one to four shocks were given during this period. On other trials the patient viewed slides of nude females that were presented as relief stimuli when he turned off a shock that was presented without warning. Finger plethysmograph records from unshocked trials were analyzed for each subject to obtain an average response for the first half and the last half of the treatment sessions. These records were intended to measure sexual responsiveness. Response to slides was typically a decrease in blood volume (vasoconstriction). Latency, amplitude, and recovery time were measured. The direction of change in treatment over sessions was toward decreasing amplitude of response for all slides, increasing recovery rate for male slides, and slightly decreasing recovery rate for female slides. Four of the five patients showed an initial greater amplitude and duration of response to male slides than to female slides. Changes were not consistent from patient to patient, nor did they show an obvious relationship to the changes in sexual orientation observed, although the treatment was not very effective for any of the five patients. The authors did not consider their technique free from effects due to confounding of anxiety with sexual responsiveness. Vasoconstriction is a "stress" or orienting response common to a wide class of stimulus situation. The changes observed in response to male stimuli do not seem indicative of the growth of a CR, since the average for five patients declined over treatment. The value and interpretation of this measure is thus still to be demonstrated.

A third class of process measures, not analogous to procedures used in animal research, are those based on questionnaires and ratings provided by the patient. Marks, *et al.* (1965) used semantic differential ratings obtained from the masochist-fetishist they treated. The ratings of several concepts changed in appropriate directions, as measured before and after therapy. Since only one patient was treated, no data on correlation between scale change and therapeutic change could be provided. Some such evidence is a necessary condition to establish the scale as a measure of therapeutic change for use in individual cases.

Other variables than those involved in therapeutic change can affect reports given by the patient. The Marks, *et al.* manner of presentation involved breaking up concepts and scales to avoid "response set," apparently conceived of as a factor that might result from specific groupings of items within the scale. The complexity of the Feldman, *et al.* scales, previously discussed, may have been intended for a similar purpose.

These scales were not designed to maintain validity in cases of deliberate faking. They were intended to provide essentially veridical reports of patient attitudes and behavior. However, biases of various sorts are consistent accompaniments of self-report scales. Important biases may be introduced by the relationship of the patient to the therapist. We have already mentioned the importance of this relationship as a contributing factor in the patient's behavior, and will discuss it in more detail later. The subtle and pervasive manner in which the situation background may affect responses to specific experimental cues has been seen repeatedly in the psychological testing literature, and influences of situational factors on reports of internal states is seen even in psychophysical studies of detection and recognition (Galanter, 1962). Subjects may well not be aware of these influences on their reports. Detection of fakery, assurance of confidentiality, and other efforts to eliminate conscious and deliberate bias may not succeed in removing the more subtle biasing influences. Thus, careful validation of the scales is required.

Relief stimuli with nonpsychotic patients. Two procedures have been used to create relief stimuli. In both cases other training was included, either aversion, escape, or avoidance. In one procedure, shocked and unshocked (relief) stimuli are intermixed in a classical conditioning procedure. In the second, unshocked (relief) stimuli are presented as a consequence of an avoidance or escape response. Examples of the first situation are: Thorpe, *et al.* (1964), Thorpe, *et al.* (1963), and Clark (1965). These studies randomly mixed trials using shocked and unshocked conditioned stimuli. No explicit response was required. The relief stimuli were, for example, female nude pinups in the Clark study.

Solyom and Miller (1965) used the second procedure described above. Intermixed with classical conditioning trials, they included other trials in which the homosexual patient would automatically produce a relief stimulus (a slide of an attractive female) by escaping from uncued shock. In a second part of the Clark study avoidance training was used. The patient could avoid shock by a sufficiently fast button press contingent on tachistoscopic presentation of the conditioned stimulus. Frequent relief stimuli were presented and not followed by shock, so that if no avoidance response was made these stimuli would remain on the screen for some time, thus delaying further trials. Patients learned to discriminate quickly, escaping or avoiding the shock contingent "pathological" stimuli, but not responding when the relief stimuli appeared. Thus relief stimuli were presumed to have become conditioned reinforcers. However, the situation was such that withholding the avoidance response when relief stimuli appeared produced time out from avoidance as well as the continuation of the relief stimulus, so that a reinforcing property of the stimulus is not demonstrated by this procedure. None of these studies have included a test of the adequacy of the procedure to produce conditioned positive reinforcers. In view of the many negative experimental results involving relief stimulus building procedures, such a demonstration is desirable.

The Feldman and MacCulloch avoidance training procedure for homosexuals used relief stimuli (slides of attractive females) presented contingent on the avoidance responses, on some trials. After the relief stimulus was discontinued it would sometimes be re-presented if the patient so requested. MacCulloch *et al.* (1965) presented some case study data on the frequency of requests for return of the relief slide. Removal of this slide was controlled by the therapist, and the duration of presentation was not stated. The request was interpreted as indicating the conditioned positive reinforcing strength of these slides. Compliance with the request not only returned the relief slide to the screen, however; it provided a time out from the avoidance procedure associated with the regular training trials, thus introducing the problem just previously discussed.

Generalized effects of aversive stimuli. Generalized changes associated with the use of aversive stimuli have been alluded to throughout this paper. In studies of nonpsychotic patients who volunteered for treatment, temporary increases in anxiety and aggressiveness have been observed in several instances, and there are several reports of patients who became so fearful that they withdrew from treatment. Some of these results may be indirect effects of aversive conditioning, such as increased arousal, or conditioning of aversion to static environmental cues, making the therapeutic situation itself aversive. An example of such generalized aversion may be seen in Oswald's (1962) procedure, which involved an essentially uncontrolled use of aversive stimuli, and which might have established aversion to almost any stimulus in the treatment setting. However, behavior changes, not anticipated as direct effects of treatment, are also frequently observed. Such changes during therapy were noted by Thorpe, *et al.* (1964). Unfortunately no controlled data on generalized effects of treatment of nonpsychotic patients have been collected in the studies reviewed here. The data available do not suggest cause for concern about lasting harmful effects from the controlled use of aversive stimuli.

More precise data are presented in Figure 2, for schizophrenic children, where, after the suppression of self-destructive behavior by aver-

sive stimuli, the child cries and fusses less and also avoids the attending
adults less. Similar findings were reported on another patient who provided the data for Figure 3. Again we see the same changes in Figure
4 where, after punishment for self-stimulation and aggression, the two
children involved spent by far the larger amount of time in close physical contact with the attending adult. The two children who provided the
data in that figure were also rated by the attending nursing personnel,
who observed the children increasing in responsivity to adults, affection-
seeking, and dependency on the adults. Some of these measures were also
recorded by the experimenters in terms of decrease in withdrawals and
increases in the child's embraces, hugs, and kisses. The filmed record of
these children during successful shock avoidance shows very dramatic
changes.[6] These two children, who seemed completely without social
behavior prior to the study, engaged in behavior during the shock sessions that had never been observed in these children before. Specifically, they seemed much more alert and visually explored their environment. They would cup and mold to the adults' bodies in what clinically
might be described as tactual hunger. Such behavior would probably
have precluded the diagnosis of autism if it had occurred upon admis-
sion to the hospital. Perhaps the most surprising finding was that during
successful shock avoidance the children seemed happy. That is, they
would look directly at the attending adult and smile in a contented manner at him as they approached him. This was the first time that these
children had been observed to give a social smile. These changes of behavior are apparent in the film record. Some of these changes, such as
the change in alertness, occurred within seconds of the aversive stimulation. Others, such as the happiness and contentment, emerged only after the children had learned the overt behaviors needed to master this
situation. It is findings like these, pertaining to the large change in emotional behavior, perceptual behavior, and potential expansion of reinforcing events, which lead one to speculate that the primary deficiency
in these children centers on inadequacy in what is referred to clinically
as anxiety.

The use of aversive stimuli, then, brings into consideration what effect such stimuli have upon the child's "mood" or emotional behavior,
and how these states mediate changes in what we consider instrumental
behavior. Investigations into these dimensions have just been started

6. The filmed record is available for viewing upon request to the authors.

(Stahelski & Lovaas, 1967) but they do suggest that the variables involved are very powerful. A good example of such power is given in a subsequent study comparing the effect of three "mood" variables on four behaviors. Specifically, the child's "mood" was varied by contrasting an everyday situation—sitting beside an adult on a chair—that we labeled a control situation, with a situation of considerable comfort—being placed in a tub of water (the water condition). The control "mood" was also compared to a situation that was noxious in the sense that the children were verbally reprimanded by a loud "no." The effect of this upon the four behaviors that we recorded are presented in Figure 12. Altogether, four children were observed, each being seen in three

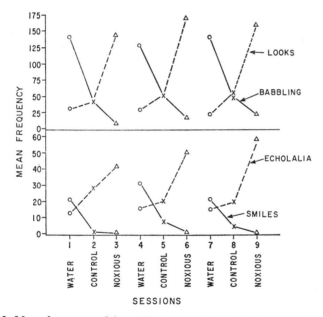

FIG. 12. Mean frequency of four different behaviors (looks, babbling, echolalia, and smiles) as a function of three different conditions (water, control, and noxious).

sessions, each session presenting the three conditions in a nonsytematic order. As can be observed, noxious stimulation suppressed smiles and babbling, while these same behaviors increased considerably in the pleasant affect (water) condition. The opposite effect can be observed in the two other behaviors, echolalic speech and looking at the adult's face. The striking feature of these data pertains to their very immediate and substantial effects. The instantaneous changes that accompany the presentation of these "affect" variables contrast markedly to the much more gradual changes which one would observe if these behaviors were, in fact, shaped by reinforcement. This conclusion should be qualified since some of these changes might be due to the discriminative stimulus properties of these variables. The main point of the study, however, speaks of the importance of considering affect variables, for example, in educational efforts.

The final study on the effects of non-contingent affect stimuli pertains to the duration of these effects upon the child's behavior. Figure 13 shows the effect of noncontingent noxious stimuli (a slap) upon spon-

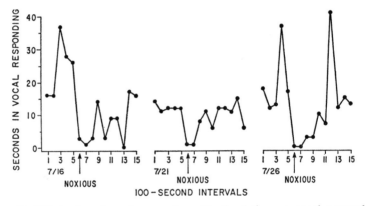

FIG. 13. Effect of noxious (non-contingent) stimulation on vocal responding. The abscissa gives number of seconds in vocal responding out of each 100-second interval. Data are gathered on three different days.

taneous vocalizations. The noxious stimuli were presented on three different days at different stages of the training sessions. The figure shows that the suppression of spontaneous vocalizations is rather temporary, apparently not exceeding 800 seconds in duration. This observation is consistent with our clinical impressions, where a more durable change in the child's mood would require much more prolonged and consistent use of affect variables.

VERBAL AND IMAGINAL STIMULI

Some studies with nonpsychotics have used verbal or imaginal stimuli, rather than actual objects, pictures, or photographs, as conditioned stimuli. This procedure is very common in systematic desensitization. Responses acquired to the symbolic stimuli are expected to generalize to stimuli in outside situations. Thorpe, *et al.* (1964) used words or phrases presented visually, to be read aloud by the patient. The patient's verbalization of the word was followed by shock. Some words, not followed by shock, were designated relief stimuli. All words dealt with the problem treated; the relief stimuli represented objects or behaviors considered acceptable and appropriate for the patient to approach or perform. For one homosexual the stimuli followed by shock were phrases in common use among homosexuals or referring to homosexual practices. For another the single word "homosexual" was shocked with "girl-friend," used as relief stimulus. For some cases, for example, a phobic patient, appropriate phrases appear to have been difficult to find; this might have resulted in less effective generalization to appropriate external situations.

Some patients have been treated using verbal stimuli only, and some studies used other stimuli in addition. Verbal stimuli used by Clark (1965) were reported by one patient as more potent than pictorial stimuli, which were also used, and the verbal stimuli aroused greater GSRs. Outcomes of studies using verbal stimuli do not obviously differ in success rate from those previously discussed, although the data are hardly decisive.

Successful outcomes observed in these studies give some indication that generalization from verbal stimuli to external stimuli may occur readily. Studies in semantic generalization, reviewed by Feather (1965), throw only scattered light on this question; available data indicate that generalization from a symbol to the object symbolized may occur, but there appear to be frequent sharp and idiosyncratic discriminations.

Patient-produced imaginal stimuli have been used in several studies, sometimes in connection with other stimuli (Thorpe, *et al.*, 1964; Kushner & Sandler, 1966; McGuire & Vallance, 1964; Mees, 1966; Marks, *et al.*, 1965). On an instruction or other cue to begin the trials the patient attempts to produce an image of a designated stimulus or activity. When the image is clear he signals for shock or administers shock to himself. Thus both the imaginal response and the signal for shock are punished. Typically, latency of the signal for shock or reported difficulty in producing images increases over trials, as would be expected of a response undergoing suppression.

If this procedure is to be effective the aversive stimulation delivered must affect more behavior than the observed latency of the overt signal for shock. However, the relevant events, such as interoceptive and proprioceptive stimulation, imaginal events, or covert verbalizations, are internal to the organism, and the difficulties involved in obtaining valid reports in this area are well known.

The extension of the terminology of the analysis of overt behavior to covert events such as thinking, imagining, and covert language has been objected to by many writers, e.g., Chomsky (1959), and defended by others (Homme, 1965). In the studies referred to here, in which a patient is punished for instructed imaginal productions, various analyses of the results of these techniques may be feasible. First, it may be supposed that the imaginal activity involves the production of "imaginary" stimuli of such a nature that respondents attached to these stimuli generalize to related external stimuli. Respondent conditioning and generalization may thus be invoked to explain observed aversiveness to these external stimuli, acquired in a context in which these stimuli were not present. A second possibility is that the "imaginary" production is an early part of a behavior sequence, of which later components are more overt, so that the effects of the punishment procedure may be ascribed to suppression of events that are early links in a pathological behavior sequence or chain.

Inability to measure the components of a process directly need not prohibit investigation of the process, if functional relations can be found between the components and observables. Some procedures useful in such investigations are shown in Kelleher's (1966) discussion of research on chaining behavior. For the aversion conditioning procedure using imaginal responses, measures of generalization to overt responding may be obtained directly. Measures of latencies, response rates, and physiological activity in the acquisition process are also available. Thus, treatment using covert events cannot be invalidated on procedural grounds, nor is a different descriptive model necessarily required than that used in the analysis of overt behavior.

THE THERAPIST AS A FACTOR IN TREATMENT

Few of the studies reviewed here have considered the role of the therapist as an active agent in treatment. Eysenck (1960, p. 11) described the therapeutic relationship as an inessential, if occasionally useful, factor in behavior therapy. In this view, behavior therapy achieves its results through application of principles of learning, not through the operation of the diffuse and not well-understood concepts such as "patient-expectations" or "therapist-effects." Behavior therapy has been criticized frequently for neglect of the therapist's role (Andrews, 1966). To these critics the behavior therapist appears to see himself unrealistically as an external observer and to ignore the contribution he may make beyond the specific techniques he uses.

The controversy involves not only the source of behavior change but also the terms appropriate for its description. On the one hand, one may investigate the question by looking at personality characteristics and general modes of interaction of the participants in therapy. On the other hand, a more useful approach may be to place the interaction within a framework involving more specific factors, such as social control and reinforcement.

Traditional therapies have usually stressed non-behavioral and rather general characteristics of the therapeutic interaction. Such factors as warmth, acceptance, interpersonal attraction and dependency are among those investigated, as recently reviewed by Goldstein, Heller, and Sechrest (1966). Koenig and Masters (1965) examined general therapist characteristics in their study. Patients rated therapists on such variables as intelligence, warmth, skill and attractiveness. Some correlations with outcome were obtained. The study does not give data useful to determine how these variables may have operated. Behavior therapy might fail, for example, if the technique is ineptly applied; a factor that may show a significant relationship to patient and therapist personality variables or to the resulting interpersonal interaction that takes place. Therapy may also fail through some more direct operation of these personality and interaction variables that considerations of technique alone do not reveal.

A reading of the reported case studies shows clearly that the relationship of the therapist and client can influence the course of a behavior therapy procedure in several ways. Oswald (1962) pointed to an important therapist function encountered in his research. The therapist's intervention was required frequently to maintain the patients cooperation during the grueling treatment, which included confinement in a room with a taped message playing insulting comments, while the patient experienced nausea from an emetic drug given approximately every 2 hours. The patient had the option of leaving the program, and

Oswald noted that the option was occasionally exercised. This eventuality would seem to be readily predictable from consideration of the technique used. Since many stages of this cooperation were followed by, or associated with, aversive stimulation, it may be expected that cooperative behavior would undergo suppression. Use of aversive stimulation may create aversion to many aspects of the treatment situation, including the therapist and the setting, even if the procedure is well controlled. One might suppose that patients who did not leave treatment received positive reinforcement for continued cooperation, or perhaps a threat of greater, if less immediate, punishment for leaving, or for thoughts of leaving. The encouragement, explanations, remarks on progress, instructions, and authoritative pronouncements of the therapist can provide such reinforcement and control.

A discussion of a similar problem is provided by Schwitzgebel (1964) for a situation that is presumably not highly aversive. He used monetary reinforcers with delinquents to shape behaviors such as prompt and regular attendance at therapy sessions. These reinforcers were mixed with therapist comments and attitudes deemed appropriate for the occasion, on the basis of a behavioral analysis of the interaction process. Analysis in these terms appears to offer a way out of some treatment problems due to failures in maintaining the delinquent in treatment, and may provide techniques for control in other situations.

Wolpe (1964) shows the potential usefulness of an analysis of the way the patient's behavior is maintained in treatment. He treated an addict using a take-home, patient-administered electric shock. The patient delivered shock to himself on the occurrence of particular thoughts, whenever these occurred. The patient also made occasional visits to the therapist. A difficulty in use of this technique is that the technique appears to be self-defeating. One may wonder why the instructed response of self-punishment, immediately preceding shock, was not suppressed, especially in view of the fact that shock appeared successful in temporarily suppressing the drug-craving response. On its face, Wolpe's technique might seem to be of very limited utility since patients would not continue to cooperate in the program. The manner in which cooperation is induced and maintained when the therapist is not present is of obvious relevance. Unfortunately, Wolpe did not comment on this problem.

Ferster, Nurnberger, and Levitt (1962) discussed the uses that the patient may make of stimulus control techniques as leverage for obtaining control of his own behavior. Some of these devices appear to require no more than a set of instructions to apply, although the extra reinforcement and control by a therapist would probably be an advantage. Ferster, *et al.* considered the patient's recognition of the results of his efforts at self-control to be the main reinforcer for their continued application. Of course, patient understanding of what results are reasonable is crucial here. Successfully following instructions provided by the therapist, or by the patient himself, may also have reinforcing value.

The examples above do not concern operant control procedures only. The therapist's ability to elicit and reinforce respondents should not be overlooked. As has been shown, an important problem in treatment of schizophrenic children is to make actions of other humans reinforcing for them. For more normal persons such reinforcement factors are usually already quite powerful. Respondent processes appear to figure prominently in conventional therapies with more normal persons. Here the emotional aspects of the patient-therapist "interaction" are usually emphasized in the various descriptive terminologies used.

The effect of these interaction variables make functional analysis of treatment procedures complex. Since most of the variables operating in social control depend on prior histories of socially significant relationships, these variables may act in less complex ways for schizophrenic children, for whom significant relationships often seem hardly to have existed, or, as in the case of Kevin, previously described, to be directly manipulable in treatment. This absence of an extensive social (or any other) learned repertoire of stimulus functions in many schizophrenic children means that control of variables in treatment is less complicated, which perhaps accounts partially for the relative ease with which behavioral measures of therapeutic effects can be obtained for these children. As treatment progresses with these children, and complex repertories of social, verbal, and intellectual behaviors develop, such precise behavioral control becomes less easily achieved.

Some Outcome Data and Final Comments

It is apparent that numerous variations of technique have been developed for the application of aversive stimulation in therapy. Specific and refined quantitative measures of progress and outcomes have been much less common. Therapeutic outcome of one sort or another provides the essential test of success of the behavior therapies as a whole, as well as for specific techniques. Examination and criticism of techniques on more general grounds, as has been attempted here, do not provide a substitute for definition and measurement of suitable outcome criteria.

It has been clear throughout that the work with nonpsychotic patients has proceeded on quite different grounds than the work with schizophrenic children. The schizophrenic children have been involved in a continuing treatment setting. Their cumulative progress has been visible, from the early training in attending to other persons and responding to elementary requests, through the acquisition of more complex skills such as spontaneous and coherent speech, reading, and a repertoire of social abilities.

Almost all the other work reported has been carried out over only a short period of time, and often involved only some "core" aspect of the problem. For example, aversion conditioning of alcoholism clearly leaves a large part of the alcoholic's behavior problems unsolved, as does aversion treatment of homosexuality, with or without concommitant training with "relief" stimuli. No doubt further therapy was provided in many of these cases, but it is seldom discussed in the reports given. For these cases then, a fully successful outcome, as measured in the life situation, requires more behavior change than is directly produced by application of controlled aversive stimulation, and thus depends on uncontrolled factors in the outside environment. We might expect to see the greatest success in those cases in which treatment is most relevant to the behavior problem, and the extra factors are minimal, as in, perhaps, enuresis and most cases of transvestism and fetishism.

The two problems that have received the greatest therapeutic effort have also received the most detailed outcome work. These are the treatment of alcoholism and enuresis. Treatment of enuresis by variations on the conditioning technique developed by Mowrer and Mowrer (1938) has provided data from many studies (Jones, 1960). Lovibond (1964) reviewed 604 cases treated and found an average success rate of 90%. Young and Turner (1965) found a success rate of 74.3% for 299 cases, including cases that did not complete the set period of treatment (14 consecutive dry nights or four months). These figures do not take into account relapse rates as determined by follow-up after treatment. Cases not considered severe, or cases with unfavorable family conditions or parental attitudes, were not taken for treatment. These figures compare quite favorably with Lovibond's (1964) reported estimates of untreated "cure" rates: 25% per year at ages 3-4, falling to 16% at ages 11-12.

Lemere and Voegtlin (1950), and Voegtlin and Broz (1949), reviewing over 4,000 cases they had treated for alcoholism, found 44% abstinent from the first treatment to the time of the survey. Abstinence, complete and continuous, from alcohol in any form was achieved for at least six months for 85% of cases treated. Of 878 relapsed patients who were retreated, 39% remained abstinent after the second treatment. Abstinence rates fell for patients observed over long periods (to about 25% for patients followed for ten years), but problems of follow-up and absence of control over the ex-patients make the long-term percentages difficult to interpret.

Among the studies that have been reviewed here, use of control groups has been rare. Control groups provide a valuable alternative to single-case study for investigation of specific manipulations. Perhaps the most extensive control group research has been done in treatment of enuresis. As an example, Young and Turner (1965) compared three variations in the treatment of enuresis, using a buzzer to awaken the child at the onset of urination. One condition used a standard procedure alone; in the other two a stimulant drug was given to the child before retiring, in addition to the standard procedure. A different drug was used in each condition. The stimulants produced a significant drop (over 50%) in the number of discontinued treatment cases, and in total "wet" nights to criterion, compared to the first (control) condition. (The two measures of the outcome are related since the procedure is demanding of the parents, and a lengthy period of treatment increases dropout rate.) However, relapse rates after 12 months were greater for one of the groups treated with a stimulant (30% compared to 13% for the other two groups). Turner and Young (1966), in a later follow-up of this work, extending the follow-up to a period of up to five years, confirmed the finding of higher relapse rates for one of the drug-treated groups. Successful retreatment of relapses is common for enuresis (Jones, 1960), so that relapses are a different class of treatment failure than cases discontinued because of parental withdrawal. However, if relapsed cases are to be included as failures in determining outcome of treatment, then it appears that the number of wet nights to a criterion is not a good predictor of outcome across treatment modifications.

Koenig and Masters (1965) compared three methods of treating smoking, one of which has been previously discussed. Patients in the other groups were given either systematic desensitization or supportive counseling. Data for 27 participants showed no clear advantage for any one treatment. At the end of six months the subjects had resumed smoking at 75-85% of pretreatment rates (average over subjects within treatment groups).

In contrast to the studies in enuresis, the Koenig and Masters study compared three versions of quite different therapies. It is difficult to see how a result that succeeded in distinguishing the therapies on an outcome criterion could be interpreted as favorable or unfavorable for the therapeutic method as a whole, given the large class of techniques represented by each of those used, except perhaps for quite dramatic differences. As has been indicated, the aversive training procedure used by Koenig and Masters contained features that might have mitigated against successful outcome. A variation of this or the other procedures might have shown better (or worse) results, but the possibilities in these variations remain undetermined. A fairly large number of careful comparisons of representative methods might give grounds for a preference between three such different approaches as were used here, but the current need appears to be for research within behavior therapeutic techniques, rather than for broad comparisons among versions of competing therapeutic doctrines and strategies.

Comparison of outcome results for the behavior therapies with successes from other therapies for similar problems encounters several difficulties. Careful data from alternative therapeutic practices has been infrequently published, and criteria for improvement are likely to be different from those common here. Discursive case studies, of which many have been reviewed here, are inadequate as a basis for determining success rates of a particular technique; yet case studies and research on small groups, using a number of procedural variations, provide the entire reported evidence for the success of behavior therapy for fetishism, transvestism, and obsessive behavior. It is likely that research in behavior therapy is more fully reported than for other therapies, since the number of practitioners has been few, and an entire journal is devoted to reporting their work. Even so, an unsuccessful effort is less likely to reach printed form than a success, and the number of failures and the techniques that failed are not known.

Currently available studies only initiate the amount of work needed to fully understand the therapeutic uses of aversive stimuli. The information to this point is encouraging, and sometimes unexpected. It is appropriate to make some final comments on the context of the work with the schizophrenic children, since the data on the effect of aversive stimulation on these children are relatively extensive and more immediately available.

The encouraging aspects of shock seem rather obvious in, for example, the case of suppression of self-destructive behavior. Here, the shock is so effective as to virtually accomplish most of the treatment within the first minute. It was surprising that it would be this effective in children who have spent so much time mutilating themselves, and inflicting so much damage and presumably pain upon themselves, as to make shock seem insignificant by comparison. A rationale for these contrasting effects of noxious stimulation lies in the novel nature of shock; shock has not had an opportunity to acquire positive reinforcing properties—it simply hurts.

One of the most unexpected findings pertained to the highly situational nature of shock. Children did not develop a generalized fear of adults; rather, they developed fears in very restricted situations (for example, when the adult looked angrily at them). Similarly, the data show unambiguously that if one suppresses behavior in one environment, then that behavior is not necessarily suppressed in another. Clinically, one would not expect this kind of discrimination and it raises serious questions for a number of short-term, removed from real-life therapeutic attempts that we have reviewed in this chapter. The findings make sense, however, if one considers the vast opportunities that the patients have for discrimination learning. As soon as the schizophrenic child, for example, steps from the experimental rooms onto the ward he experiences different contingencies unless the experimental environment is extended to include that ward. Similarly, the adults who care for these children obviously not only punish them, but also provide adequate discrimination learning in the sense that they will be very content and happy with the children when they play with them, feed them, and so on. An adult thus becomes not just one, but rather many persons to the child, in the sense of being many stimuli. The same reasoning, of course, can be applied to the child. The child is not one unit, or one "person." The child is a large number of behaviors, as many as he has environments. When we argue that the child is a function of his environment we might better say that he is a function of his environments, because children are vastly different from one environment to another. This is particularly apparent in the data presented here, where the environments have been made different by presenting noxious stimuli in one, and withholding them in another.

We have talked so far about some of the effects and side effects of aversive stimuli on the individuals who receive them. It is appropriate at this point to comment briefly on the effects of the use of aversive stimuli on the therapists who apply them. It is easy to love sick patients and children. It is an almost compelling "natural instinct," so to speak, to reassure, comfort, and support them. We attach no particular achievement to these feelings, but consider them part of every person's repertoire as a human being. It is another matter altogether whether, when seeking to satisfy one's own needs to give love, one is also helpful to the recipient of that love. Our data strongly suggest that expressions of love, contingent upon self-destructive behavior in children, are exactly what keep the patients tied down in restraints. It seems that the giving of such love may benefit the giver, but not the receiver. We did not expect this finding. Just as it is very easy to love sick persons (it is easier, often, to love a sick person than a normal, healthy, cantankerous one), it is difficult to punish the sick. Of the many people who have been involved in administering punishment to children in the UCLA project, perhaps some 40 or 50 staff members by this time, all have approached the task with extreme reluctance and anxiety.

No doubt the ethics of today's world instigate a great deal of this anxiety. The same ethics, however, also give rise to the experience of much responsibility for the child by the person who administers punishment. It is somewhat strange that if treatment goes wrong for a therapist who "loves" the patient, he is likely to be held less responsible for that outcome than as if he punished him. It is probable that this increased sense of responsibility is related to the awareness that in using aversive stimuli one is operating with very powerful variables. The use of powerful variables in treatment makes a therapist more directly recognize his responsibility for the therapeutic outcome and less likely to employ terms such as "freeing the patient," or "encouraging the innate need to become healthy." In working with schizophrenic children at UCLA we look upon use of such constructs as delegation of responsibility, that is, as attempts to avoid making the kinds of decisions, assuming the kind of control, and therefore by necessity using the kinds of powerful variables that are needed in order to make the difference.

REFERENCES

Andrews, J. D. W. Psychotherapy of phobias. *Psychological Bulletin*, 1966, **66**, 455–480.

Azrin, N. H., & Holz, W. C. Punishment. In W. K. Honig (Ed.), *Operant Behavior*. New York: Appleton-Century-Crofts, 1966.

Beck, R. C. On secondary reinforcement and shock termination. *Psychological Bulletin*, 1961, **58**, 28–45.

Berger, S. M. Conditioning through vicarious instigation. *Psychological Review*, 1962, **69**, 450–466.

Blake, B. G. The application of behaviour therapy to the treatment of alcoholism. *Behavior Research and Therapy*, 1965, **3**, 75–85.

Blakemore, C. B. The application of behavior therapy to a sexual disorder. In H. J. Eysenck and S. Rachman (Eds.), *Experiments in behavior therapy*. Oxford: Pergamon Press, 1964.

Blakemore, C. B., Thorpe, J. G., Barker, J. C., Conway, C. G., & Lavin, N. I. The application of faradic aversion conditioning in a case of transvestism. *Behavior Research and Therapy*, 1963, **1**, 29–34.

Chomsky, N. Review of B. F. Skinner, *Verbal behavior*. *Language*, 1959, **35**, 26–58.

Clark, D. F. A note on avoidance conditioning techniques in sexual disorders. *Behavior Research and Therapy*, 1965, **3**, 203–206.

Dinsmoor, J. A., & Clayton, Marilyn H. A conditioned reinforcer maintained by temporal association with the termination of shock. *Journal of the Experimental Analysis of Behavior*, 1966, **9**, 547–556.

Eysenck, H. J. *Behavior therapy and the neuroses*. New York: Macmillan, 1960.

Feather, B. W. Semantic generalization of classically conditioned responses: a review. *Psychological Bulletin*, 1965, **63**, 425–441.

Feldman, M. P., & MacCulloch, M. J. The application of anticipatory avoidance learning to the treatment of homosexuality. I. Theory, technique, and preliminary results. *Behavior Research and Therapy*, 1964, **2**, 165–183.

Feldman, M. P., MacCulloch, M. J., Mellor, V., & Pinschof, J. M. The application of anticipatory avoidance learning to the treatment of homosexuality. III. The sexual orientation method. *Behavior Research and Therapy*, 1966, **4**, 289–300.

Ferster, C. B. Positive reinforcement and behavioral deficits of autistic children. *Child Development*, 1961, **32**, 437–456.

Ferster, C. B., Nurnberger, J. I., & Levitt, E. B. The control of eating. *Journal of Mathematics*, 1962, **1**, 87–110.

Franks, C. M. Alcohol, alcoholism and conditioning: a review of the literature and some theoretical considerations. *Journal of Medical Science*, 1958, **104**, 14–33.

Franks, C. M., Fried, R., & Ashem, B. An improved apparatus for the aversive conditioning of cigarette smokers. *Behavior Research and Therapy*, 1966, **4**, 301–308.

Freund, K. Some problems in the treatment of homosexuality. In H. J. Eysenck (Ed.), *Behavior therapy and the neuroses*. Oxford: Pergamon Press, 1960.

Galanter, E. Contemporary psychophysics. In T. M. Newcomb (Ed.), *New directions in psychology*. New York: Holt, Rinehart and Winston, 1962.

Glynn, J. D., & Harper, D. Behavior therapy in transvestism. *Lancet*, 1961, **4**, 619.

Goldstein, A. P., Heller, K., & Sechrest, L. B. *Psychotherapy and the psychology of behavior change*. New York: John Wiley, 1966.

Hitzing, E. W., & Risley, T. *Elimination of self-destructive behavior in a retarded girl by noxious stimulation*. Atlanta: Southwestern Psychological Association, 1967.

Homme, L. E. Perspectives in psychology: XXIV. Control of coverants, the operants of the mind. *Psychological Record*, 1965, **15**, 501–511.

James, B. A case of homosexuality treated by aversion therapy. *British Medical Journal*, 1962, **1**, 768–770.

Jones, H. G. The behavioral treatment of enuresis nocturna. In H. J. Eysenck (Ed.), *Behavior therapy and the neuroses*. New York: Macmillan, 1960.

Kamin, L. J. Temporal and intensity characteristics of the CS. In W. F. Prokasy (Ed.), *Classical conditioning: a symposium*. New York: Appleton-Century-Crofts, 1965.

Kamin, L. J., & Schaub, R. E. Effects of conditioned stimulus intensity on the conditioned emotional response. *Journal of Comparative and Physiological Psychology*, 1963, **56**, 502–507.

Kelleher, R. T. Chaining and conditioned reinforcement. In W. K. Honig (Ed.), *Operant behavior*. New York: Appleton-Century-Crofts, 1966.

Koenig, K. P., & Masters, J. Experimental treatment of habitual smoking. *Behavior Research and Therapy*, 1965, **3**, 235–244.

Kushner, M., & Sandler, J. Aversion therapy and the concept of punishment. *Behavior Research and Therapy*, 1966, **4**, 179–186.

Kushner, M. Faradic control in clinical practice. *Ninth annual institute for research in clinical psychology*. University of Kansas, in press.

Lavin, N. I., Thorpe, J. G., Barker, J. C., Blakemore, G. B., & Conway, C. G. Behavior therapy in a case of transvestism. *Journal of Nervous and Mental Diseases*, 1961, **33**, 346–353.

Lemere, F., & Voegtlin, W. L. An evaluation of the aversion treatment of alcoholism. *Quarterly Journal of Studies on Alcohol*, 1950, **11**, 199–204.

Liversedge, L. A., & Sylvester, J. D. Conditioning techniques in the treatment of writer's cramp. *Lancet*, 1955, 1147–1149.

Lovaas, O. I. A behavior therapy approach to the treatment of childhood schizophrenia. In J. Hill (Ed.), *Minnesota symposium on child psychology*. University of Minnesota Press, 1967.

Lovaas, O. I., Freitag, G., Gold, Vivian J., & Kassorla, Irene C. Experimental studies in childhood schizophrenia: analysis of self-destructive behavior. *Journal of Experimental Child Psychology,* 1965, **2**, 67–84. (a)

Lovaas, O. I., Freitag, G., Gold, Vivian J., & Kassorla, Irene C. A recording method and observations of behaviors of normal and autistic children in free play settings. *Journal of Experimental Child Psychology,* 1965, **2**, 108–120. (b)

Lovaas, O. I., Schaeffer, B., & Simmons, J. Q. Experimental studies in childhood schizophrenia: building social behavior in autistic children by use of electric shock. *Journal of Experimental Research in Personality,* 1965, **1**, 99–109. (c)

Lovibond, S. H. *Conditioning and enuresis.* New York: Macmillan, 1964.

Lovibond, S. H. The mechanism of conditioning treatment of enuresis. *Behavior Research and Therapy,* 1963, **1**, 17–21.

McAllister, W. R., & McAllister, D. E. Variables influencing the conditioning and the measurement of acquired fear. In W. R. Prokasy (Ed.), *Classical conditioning: a symposium.* New York: Appleton-Century-Crofts, 1965.

MacCulloch, M. J., Feldman, M. P., Orford, J. F., & MacCulloch, M. L. Anticipatory avoidance learning in the treatment of alcoholism: a record of therapeutic failure. *Behavior Research and Therapy,* 1966, **4**, 187–196.

MacCulloch, M. J., Feldman, M. P., & Pinschof, J. M. The application of anticipatory avoidance learning to the treatment of homosexuality. II. Avoidance response latencies and pulse rate changes. *Behavior Research and Therapy,* 1965, **3**, 21–44.

McGuire, R. J., & Vallance, M. Aversion therapy by electric shock: a simple technique. *British Medical Journal,* 1964, **1**, 151–153.

Marks, I. M., Rachman, S., & Gelder, M. G. Methods for assessment of avoidance training in fetishism and masochism. *Behavior Research and Therapy,* 1963, **1**, 253–258.

Marx, M. H. Differential resistance to extinction of escape and avoidance conditioning. *Psychological Record,* 1966, **16**, 449–456.

Mees, H. L. Sadistic fantasies modified by aversive conditioning and substitution: a case study. *Behavior Research and Therapy,* 1966, **4**, 317–320.

Miller, E. C., Dvorak, B. A., & Turner, D. W. A method of creating aversion to alcohol by reflex conditioning in a group setting. *Quarterly Journal of Studies on Alcohol,* 1960, **21**, 424–431.

Morgenstern, F. S., Pearce, J. F., & Rees, W. L. Predicting the outcome of behavior therapy by psychological tests. *Behavior Research and Therapy,* 1965, **2**, 191–200.

Mowrer, O. H. *Learning theory and the symbolic process.* New York: John Wiley & Sons, 1950.

Mowrer, O. H., & Aiken, E. G. Contiguity vs. drive-reduction in conditioned fear: temporal variations in conditioned and unconditioned stimulus. *American Journal of Psychology.* 1954, **67**, 26–38.

Mowrer, O. H., & Mowrer W. M. Enuresis: a method for its study and treatment. *American Journal of Orthopsychiatry,* 1938, **8**, 436–459.

Oswald, I. Introduction of illusory and hallucinatory voices with consideration of behavior therapy. *Journal of Mental Science,* 1962, **108,** 196–212.

Rachman, S. Aversion therapy: chemical or electrical? *Behavior Research and Therapy,* 1964, **2,** 289–299.

Raymond, M. A case of fetishism treated by aversion therapy. *British Medical Journal,* 1956, **2,** 854–856.

Raymond, M. The treatment of addiction by aversion conditioning with apomorphine. *Behavior Research and Therapy,* 1963, **1,** 287–292.

Raymond, M., & O'Keeffe, K. A case of pin-up fetishism treated by aversion therapy. *British Journal of Psychiatry,* 1965, **111,** 579–581.

Risley, T. *The effects and "side-effects" of the use of punishment with an autistic child.* Washington, D.C.: American Psychological Association, 1967.

Schwitzgebel, R. *Street corner research: an experimental approach to the juvenile delinquent.* Cambridge, Mass.: Harvard University Press, 1964.

Solomon, R. C., & Brush, E. S. Experimentally derived conceptions of anxiety and aversion. In M. R. Jones (Ed.), *Nebraska symposium on motivation.* Lincoln: University of Nebraska Press, 1956.

Solomon, R. C., & Wynne, L. C. Traumatic avoidance learning: acquisition in normal dogs. *Psychological Monographs,* 1953, **67,** No. 4 (Whole No. 354).

Solomon, R. L. Punishment. *American Psychologist,* 1964, **19,** 239–253.

Solomon, R. L., & Turner, L. H. Discriminative classical conditioning in dogs paralysed by curare can later control discriminative avoidance responses in the normal state. *Psychological Review,* 1962, **69,** 202–219.

Solyom, L., & Miller, S. A differential conditioning procedure as the initial phase of the behavior therapy of homosexuality. *Behavior Research and Therapy,* 1965, **3,** 147–161.

Stahelski, A. J., & Lovaas, O. I. *Two studies to increase spontaneity in autistic children.* San Francisco: Western Psychological Association, 1967.

Sylvester, J. D., & Leversedge, L. A. Conditioning and the occupational cramps. In H. J. Eysenck (Ed.), *Behavior therapy and the neuroses.* New York: Macmillan, 1960.

Tate, B. G., & Baroff, G. S. Aversive control of self injurious behavior in a psychotic boy. *Behavior Research and Therapy,* 1966, **4,** 281–287.

Thorpe, J. G., & Schmidt, E. Therapeutic failure in a case of aversion therapy. *Behavior Research and Therapy,* 1963, **1,** 293–296.

Thorpe, J. G., Schmidt, E., Brown, P. T., & Castell, D. Aversion—relief therapy: a new method for general application. *Behavior Research and Therapy,* 1964, **2,** 71–82.

Thorpe, J. G., Schmidt, T. E., & Castell, D. A comparison of positive and negative (aversive) conditioning in the treatment of homosexuality. *Behavior Research and Therapy,* 1963, **1,** 357–361.

Turner, L. H., & Solomon, R. C. Human traumatic learning: theory and experiments on the operant-respondent distinction and failures to learn. *Psychological Monographs,* 1962, **76** (Whole No. 559).

Turner, R. K., & Young, G. C. CNS stimulant drugs and conditioning treatment of nocturnal enuresis: a long term follow-up study. *Behavior Research and Therapy*, 1966, **4**, 225–228.

Verhave, T. The functional properties of a time out from an avoidance schedule. *Journal of the Experimental Analysis of Behavior*, 1962, **5**, 391–422.

Voegtlin, W. L., & Broz, W. R. The conditioned reflex treatment of chronic alcoholism. X. Analysis of 3125 admissions. *Annals of Internal Medicine*, 1949, **30**, 580–597.

Voegtlin, W. L., & Lemere, F. The treatment of alcoholism by establishing a conditioned reflex. *American Journal of Mental Science*, 1940, **199**, 802–809.

Wilde, G. J. S. Behaviour therapy for addicted cigarette smokers: a preliminary report. *Behavior Research and Therapy*, 1964, **2**, 107–109.

Wolf, M., Risley, T., & Mees, H. Application of operant conditioning procedures to the behavior problems of an autistic child. *Behavior Research and Therapy*, 1964, **1**, 305–312.

Wolpe, J. Conditioned inhibition of craving in drug addiction: a pilot experiment. *Behavior Research and Therapy*, 1964, **2**, 285–288.

Young, G. C., & Turner, R. K. CNS stimulant drugs and conditioning treatment of nocturnal enuresis. *Behavior Research and Therapy*, 1965, **3**, 93–101.